Philosophy

Shamik Chakravarty is Assistant Professor of Philosophy at Alliance University, Bangalore. His work is focused in metaphysics and philosophy of fiction. He holds a Master's in Philosophy from St. Stephen's College, University of Delhi; a Master's in Linguistics from Calcutta University; and a PhD in Philosophy from Lingnan University, Hong Kong. Shamik's previous assignments included teaching English, creative writing and philosophy, and he was associated with Sterling Publishers, where he wrote books for children and worked in Public Relations.

At Alliance University, he teaches philosophy and the MA Creative Writing Program. In his free time, he loves playing tennis.

Quick and Concise

PHILOSOPHY

Shamik Chakravarty

hachette INDIA

First published in 2025 by Hachette India
(Registered name: Hachette Book Publishing India Pvt. Ltd)
An Hachette UK company
www.hachetteindia.com

ISBN 978-93-5731-715-3

Hachette Book Publishing India Pvt. Ltd
4th/5th Floors, Corporate Centre,
Plot No. 94, Sector 44, Gurugram 122003, India

Typeset in Cambria 10/12 by Avishek Bhattacharya

Printed and bound in India
by Thomson Press India Ltd.

MIX
Paper | Supporting responsible forestry
FSC® C010615

To

Mummy, Priya and Ipshita.

Contents

GETTING STARTED

What is Philosophy?

One of the reasons I became a philosopher is that, as I proudly tell people who ask me, one of the few things in life I can do well, or at least decently enough, is to argue. I don't have the patience of a lawyer to wade through lines and lines of laws, so I decided to become a philosopher. Unlike what a lot of people might think, philosophers aren't the gurus who have written fancy books on spirituality or self-discovery that you can find in the self-help or even philosophy sections at a bookstore. So, what do philosophers do?

One major thing they do is to use arguments to examine basic views and concepts that we have about the world around us, including those that people bring into different disciplines. These can involve questions ranging from whether the abortion of a foetus is morally acceptable, whether capital punishment is right, and if euthanasia is moral to whether we have free will, what beauty or art is, what makes an action good, what is the meaning of life, what can we know and whether God exists. You can have immediate, practical questions, like whether sex through hook-ups is morally acceptable, to political ones, like what is a just way in which society can be arranged. There are really abstract questions about the nature of the mind, knowledge, truth, causation and explanation to questions at the borders of science about what distinguishes science from non-science. Additionally, when philosophers look at stuff like free will, causation and the mind, they're not only examining concepts but also discovering the nature of the world in the process.

Now a lot of people have views and even reasons for some or all of the issues above. But unlike the common person, philosophers have extensive tools to reason with, which they use to attempt to answer these questions systematically through rigorous argumentation. This is what distinguishes philosophy from self-help and religion books on the bookshelf (unless it's written by a religious philosopher who is arguing their case).

Philosophers also examine claims that are confused in various areas of life and attempt to clarify them. For instance, people say that we can harm or help the environment. But to this, it may be replied that[i] the only sort of thing that can be helped or harmed is the kind of thing for whom things can be better or worse. If that sort of thing is helped, then things can be better for it. If it can be harmed, then things can go worse for it. And things can only be better or worse for someone with a point of view. It's kind of baffling how a rock can have a point of view. If it doesn't, then how can it be helped or harmed. To this, someone might reply that the entire earth is like a system with a point of view, but this just seems metaphorical. At best, humans and animals can be harmed or helped, not the environment as such, and we only metaphorically help the environment so long as it helps humans and animals. Even whether animals have rights and their pain is morally relevant is itself a philosophical question.

My favourite conception of philosophy is from one of the most prominent philosophers of the twentieth century, Wilfrid Sellars (1912–1989). He said, 'The aim of philosophy, abstractly formulated, is to understand how things in the broadest possible sense of the term hang together in the broadest possible sense of the term.'[ii] One way to look at this is to think that philosophy tries to see how disciplines like psychology, biology, physics, history, etc., relate to each other and to form a picture of the world and what it is to be human in relation to that. That would also involve thinking about how a discipline fits into the bigger picture and the intellectual landscape, which would involve reflecting on the methods and techniques of each discipline as well.

One problem that comes up in creating this holistic picture is that there are two conflicting visions of the world – the conflict between the manifest image and the scientific image. The manifest image is our ordinary way of thinking about ourselves in the world as persons who are agents with desires, thinking and acting in the world. This is the framework within which we humans came to think of ourselves as objects amongst other objects in the world. This image consists of objects like humans, animals, plants, insects, rivers and stones. The scientific image is that of forces and theoretical entities that aren't directly observable, which sciences and social sciences postulate to explain how the world works. These can be neurobiological mechanisms, economic forces, stuff like quarks in physics and the like. For the scientific image, the table that we ordinarily see as being coloured and having no spaces in between is, as the physicist Arthur Eddington put it, '...mostly emptiness, mostly emptiness. Sparsely scattered in that emptiness are numerous electric charges rushing about with great speed; but their combined bulk amounts to less than a billionth of the bulk of the table itself.'[iii]

The manifest image has a picture of us humans as rational, having free will (that is, being the cause of our own actions and being in control of them) and morality exists at this level: actions are good or bad. At the level of the scientific image, the world is conceived as not having any value (gravity in and of itself cannot be good or bad for physics). Our actions are caused by prior causes as per the laws of nature. As a result, we ourselves don't cause them; the laws of nature control us, and we seem to lack freedom, responsibility and rationality.

Now according to Sellars, the task of philosophy is to reconcile these two images, like two of our eyes bring together each distinct two-dimensional image on the retina into a single three-dimensional one, giving rise to stereoscopic vision. Let me give an example of attempts at reconciliation of these two images in the famous mind–body problem.

The Mind–Body Problem

The mind–body problem is the question of how the mind relates to the body. Let's look at René Descartes (pronounced dey-kaat) (1596–1650), who articulated a view known as substance dualism. Substance dualism ('substance' means a thing that has properties) is the view that the mind is a different sort of thing than the body. Each has different essential properties, an essential property being a property without which an object cannot be that thing. For instance, something cannot be a triangle without it being a closed plane figure with three sides. That's the essential property of a triangle. So for Descartes, the essence of the body is matter, which is in space and has extension (length, breadth, depth), and the essence of the mind is thought, which isn't extended in space. Remember, for Descartes, thought includes whatever one can be aware of in oneself and not only rational thinking but also imagining, willing, doubting, understanding and even feeling and sensations.

Descartes' reasoning is as follows. Descartes imagines the possibility of an evil demon systematically deceiving him (we'll meet the evil demon again later in the book). Now given this possibility, I can doubt that I don't have a body since the evil demon might be deceiving me into thinking that I have a body by creating in me the experience of a body. But even then, I can't doubt that I exist. Because if I doubt that I exist, in doubting I am still thinking. And you can't think without a thinker. So I can't doubt that I exist (this is the famous *cogito, ergo sum* – 'I think, therefore I am'). And since there can't be thoughts without a mind, I can't doubt that I have a mind. How does this show that the mind and body are distinct substances?

To show that two objects are distinct, we can show that they have different properties. A triangle is different from a square because it has three sides rather than four. The Principle of the Indiscernibility of Identicals (Leibniz's Law) is that for any A and B, if A=B (that is, for A to be identical with B), then A has the same properties as B. If they have different properties, then A and B aren't identical. (Descartes didn't know the name of the principle, but his argument works on the principle.) So Descartes' argument for the dualism of mind and body is as follows: the mind has the property of *being the existence of which I cannot doubt* (like a circular table has the property of *being round*) and the body has the property of *being the existence of which I can doubt*. Thus, since they don't have the same properties, the mind is not identical to the body and are two different things.

We can now see how Descartes tries to give a complete picture by attempting to reconcile the manifest and scientific images through the dualism of mind and body. The body, being made of matter, in Descartes' view is subject to the laws of nature and part of the chain of cause and effect. The mind isn't subject to these laws, and that's how we can have free actions. The manifest image is explained through the workings of the mind and the scientific image through the body. You have a single picture of the world now, with both the mind and body as distinct substances.

The problem with Descartes' view is that it cannot explain how the mind causes actions of the body, that is, how the mind interacts with the body. Princess Elisabeth of Bohemia (1618–1680) was the first one to articulate the mind–body problem in her response to Descartes. Her point was: How can the mind, which is not in space and has no shape, come into contact with and causally interact with something that is in space and has shape? This seems mysterious. When we watch ghosts in movies, too, the proper thing is for them to pass through walls and not be able to speak with people. If they existed, that's how it would be.

Another way to reconcile the scientific and the manifest image is to say that the things we experience as part of the manifest image are identical to things as conceived in the scientific image. For instance, we say that the water that we drink and taste is identical to H_2O. When it comes to the mind–body problem, philosophers like J.J.C. Smart said that each type of mental state (every type of pain, for instance) is identical to a type of brain state (all pain is identical to some pattern of neural firing). This way, there's no problem of interaction, like dualism, since a mental state is a brain state and not separate from it. This theory is called the type identity theory.

A major objection to this theory was by the philosopher Hilary Putnam. If pain is identical to a certain type of brain state (let's say it is identical to activation in specific parts of the brain). But animals can experience pain, and yet, it may not be identical to activation in the same way. And suppose there are aliens with silicon-based brains or AI (in the future), pain for them would not be identical to the same physical state as humans. Pain isn't just realizable in one type of brain state but multiply realizable. The type identity theory therefore suffers from anthropocentrism. If we see it through Sellar's lens, it is inadequate in reconciling aspects of the manifest image with the scientific image.

Putnam came up with another view called functionalism, which is the most popular view in philosophy and cognitive science. This doesn't try to explain a mental state like pain in terms of what it is made up of, like we saw with type identity theory, but in terms of its function. A chair can be made of wood or steel, but a chair is something whose function is for us to sit in. Similarly, a mental state is a state of an organism that plays a type of role or function: given some causes, the state has typical effects. Pain is a state in an organism caused by harm to the body, and the effect can be a withdrawal from the object that caused pain. Or it can be a wince. In humans, pain then can be realized as states in certain parts of the brain that play this role, while in animals, it can be a different sort of activation.

This does seem to deal with the problem of multiple realizability, but functionalism faces the hard problem of consciousness. Consciousness is defined as what it is like to be something (in the philosopher Thomas Nagel's phrase), that is, the subject experience that is private to someone. It is something it is like to be you and something it is like to be a bat. There is a way you taste something, and that is private to you, or the way you experience the redness of red.

Functionalism faces the hard problem of consciousness: How can objective reality, like neurons firing in the brain, explain consciousness, which is subjective? How do electrochemical processes in brain cells (which are dark inside) give rise to inner feels that are lit up? How does something objective, which we can measure and with size and shape and weight (from the third person point of view) give rise to private subjective experience (first person), which on the face of it seems immeasurable?

And since the hard problem of consciousness exists, we still have the mind–body problem with us. It seems to me that this problem is due to the problem of reconciling the manifest with the scientific image. That's why there's still a philosophical task that remains to solve the hard problem of consciousness. Science, too, helps.

In this book, I carry on with Sellars's conception of philosophy. The manifest image, as we saw, was common sense. But it is also common sense constantly refining itself by making arguments, defining things, thinking of thought experiments, like the one with the evil demon we saw above, and using correlational and statistical techniques on what is directly observable. I try to bring out arguments based on common sense intuitions, but I also line them with empirical observations to refine the manifest image. I also use the rich tradition of Indian philosophy to shed light on the matter.

A lot of the problems that we see, if not all, arise due to the conflict of the manifest image and the scientific image. The problem of the meaning of life arises because why should my life have meaning if there is no value, purpose and meaning in the picture of the world given in the scientific image. We shall see this in other issues, too. As a result, we shall see that philosophy is trying to refine the manifest image, as well as trying to come up with a composite picture of the world and our place in it.

A lot has been said about philosophy, and some arguments have been given, too. But what is an argument?

Arguments

You have probably guessed that an argument is not a quarrel or a shouting match. An argument is a set of statements in which some of the statements, called premises, are given as reasons for another statement, called a conclusion. Arguments are given when we're giving reasons to support a claim, belief or even an action. We can arrange arguments into what is called standard form, in which we label the premises and add a conclusion like this.

Premise 1: If you want to make lots of friends, you need to go to school.

Premise 2: You want to make lots of friends.

Conclusion: Therefore, you need to go to school.

This is an argument that might explain to a child who doesn't want to go to school why she needs to go to school (of course, in real life we might not say it like this).

A valid argument is one in which, if all the premises are true, it is not possible for the conclusion to be false. To get this clear, let's look at these two arguments.

Premise 1: If I throw the ball at the window, the glass will break.

Premise 2: I throw the ball at the window.

Conclusion: The glass will break.

The 'if… then' statement in Premise 1 is called a conditional statement, and the first part of the statement after 'if' is called the antecedent, and the part after 'then' is the consequent. Now even if the antecedent and the consequent are false, that is, even if I never throw the ball and the window doesn't break, I have made a valid argument. Because if I had thrown the ball at the window and it is true that if I throw the ball at the window, the glass will break, then it is impossible for the conclusion to be false. We say then that the conclusion follows from the premises. An argument is valid when there is no situation in which the premises are true and the conclusion is false. The above argument is of the form:

If P then Q.

P

Therefore Q.

An argument of this pattern is called *modus ponens*. We affirm the antecedent of the conditional statement, if P then Q, by saying, yes, P is true in the second line. As a result, therefore Q.

Another common form of a valid argument is *modus tollens. For instance*:

Premise 1: If I throw the ball, the window will break.

Premise 2: The window did not break.

Conclusion: Therefore, I didn't throw the ball.

This is valid. Because throwing the ball would definitely have broken the window and since it didn't break, I didn't throw it.

Modus tollens arguments are of the form:

If P then Q.

Not-Q

Therefore, Not-P

To understand validity more clearly, it's helpful if we consider invalidity. Consider another argument:

Premise 1: If I throw the ball at the window, the glass will break.

Premise 2: The glass broke.

Conclusion: I threw the ball at the window.

This is an invalid argument. Because if the premises are true, the conclusion might be false. If Premise 1 is true and it is true that the glass broke, then it doesn't follow that I threw the ball at the window. Even if I didn't throw the ball, the glass might have broken because someone hit it with a stick. There is a possible situation where the premises are true but the conclusion is false. That's why the argument is invalid. An argument is invalid when it is possible for the conclusion to be false when the premises are true. The invalid argument above is of the form:

If P then Q

Q

Therefore P

This is a formal fallacy. A fallacy is a flaw in reasoning, and a formal fallacy is a fallacy that is due to the form or structure of the argument. Fallacies due to the content of the argument are called informal fallacies, and we'll come across some of them as we proceed. This is called the fallacy of affirming the consequent. Another formal fallacy is the fallacy of denying the antecedent seen in the argument below:

Premise 1: If you are a barber, you have cut someone's hair.

Premise 2: You are not a barber.

Conclusion: Therefore, you have not cut someone's hair.

The argument is invalid because it is possible for there to be a situation where the premises are true and I'm a philosopher, not a barber, but I have cut my cousin's hair as a kid while she was sleeping (and got a massive scolding for it!). So it's possible for the premises to be true and the conclusion to be false. The fallacy of denying the antecedent is of the form:

If P then Q.

Not-P

Therefore, Not-Q.

We can see that it doesn't matter for validity that the premises are actually true. This allows us to make predictions about possible situations. For instance, if I reason that if my opponent looks left, he will hit the ball to the right. This is valid, and even if my opponent doesn't look left during the match, I know that if he does, he will hit the ball to the right. The following is a valid argument even though all the premises are false and so is the conclusion:

Premise 1: If I am rich, I will go to Mars.

Premise 2: I am rich.

Conclusion: Therefore, I will go to Mars.

On the other hand, an argument with all the premises that are true in the actual world and which is also valid at the same time is called a sound argument.

Let's look at an argument for the existence of God called the Kalam Cosmological Argument.

Whatever begins to exist has a cause.

The universe began to exist.

Therefore, the universe has a cause.[iv]

We can formulate it as a *modus ponens* argument.

Premise 1: If something begins to exist, then it has a cause.

Premise 2: The universe is something that begins to exist.

Conclusion: Therefore, the universe has a cause. (*Modus Ponens*, Premise 1, Premise2)

The cause of the universe in this case is identified with God as the most likely explanation. In philosophy, one reason standard form helps is because the structure becomes clear, and we can see if it is valid or not. But another reason why putting arguments in standard form is useful is because we can see which of the premises might be faulty. In effect, we check whether the argument is sound. For instance, one way to question premise 2 might be to look at scientific evidence that shows that the universe didn't have a beginning.

Now consider Descartes' argument for substance dualism.

Premise 1: If my mind has the property of *being the existence of which cannot* be doubted and my body has the property of *being the existence of which can be doubted*, then my body and my mind have distinct properties.

Premise 2: My mind has the property of *being the existence of which cannot be doubted*, and my body has the property of *being the existence of which can be doubted*.

Conclusion 1: Therefore, my body and my mind have distinct properties. (*Modus ponens*, Premise 1, Premise2)

Premise 3: If the mind=the body, then they have the same property.

Conclusion 2: Therefore, the mind≠the body. (*Modus tollens*, Conclusion 1, Premise 3)

The first thing to notice in the above argument is that Conclusion 1 is an intermediate conclusion. An intermediate conclusion is a statement in an argument that is supported by premises that give reasons for it. But it also serves as a further premise for another conclusion. The other thing to notice is the form of the first three statements:

If P and Q, then R.

P and Q

Therefore R

This is *modus ponens*, too, since the variable can be a placeholder for a simple sentence without a connective that joins sentences such as and, or, not and if... then (called an atomic sentence). But it is also a placeholder for complex sentences with the connectives, too.

In the case of Descartes' argument, the problem was not seen with the premises (although they have been found to be faulty by philosophers) but with the conclusion that the mind isn't identical to the body. We saw that it suffers from the problem of interaction.

Deductive and Inductive Arguments

Right now, we are dealing with deductive arguments. For deductively valid arguments, we can find that truth is preserved from the premises to the conclusion, so they are called truth-preserving arguments. If the premises are true, the conclusion has to be true and cannot possibly be false. Deductive arguments are given to guarantee the truth of the conclusion given the premises.

But another way we reason is using inductive arguments, the form of reasoning where the argument is meant to support the likelihood of the conclusion but not guarantee it. Inductive arguments aren't truth-preserving. The conclusion might be false even though it is likely. It is highly likely that I will wake up and go to work tomorrow. But it is still possible that I don't go to work since I might get sick.

Deductive arguments can only be valid or invalid, and there are no degrees of validity. But inductive arguments can be strong or weak, and there can be degrees of strength. So I can argue that:

It has rained in Bengaluru in January 2013.

It has rained in Bengaluru in January 2014.

It has rained in Bengaluru in January 2015.

Therefore, it is likely that it will rain in Bengaluru in January

2016.

The argument can be further strengthened by citing more and more years in the past. Still, it will not guarantee the truth of the conclusion because it is still possible for there to be a drought in 2016.

We'll see a lot of reasoning and other fallacies as we go through philosophical issues in the book. For now, let's end with an issue that is more relatable.

Relativism about Truth

You might have seen people saying things like, 'This is my truth.' It looks like they're merely describing their experience. In that case, it really isn't their truth but THE truth about their experience, which is not different from the truth that the earth revolves around the sun.

But you still have people saying that there is no such thing as the truth, but truth is subjective and only relative to cultures or to your and my perspective. What does this mean?

When we say that something is relative, it means that it varies from person to person or across cultures. Something is absolute when it is constant and doesn't vary between people or societies. Relative to me, the jackfruit ice cream is tasty. Relative to my wife, who doesn't like jackfruit, the jackfruit ice cream isn't tasty. The jackfruit ice cream is not tasty per se; it is only tasty for people at times. My wife and I aren't really disagreeing.

So when people say that truth is relative, they say that there is no such thing as truth full stop; there is only truth for people at times. According to the relativist, when someone says it is true for me that the earth revolves around the sun and another person says that it is true for me that the sun revolves around the earth, they aren't contradicting each other. If one person was saying the earth revolves around the sun and the other that it is not the case that the earth revolves around the sun, that would be a contradiction. But adding 'for me' after each

> **Proposition:** A proposition is the meaning that sentences saying the same thing have in common. Suppose in German, someone says, '*Es regnet*,' in Hindi, '*Baarish ho rahi hai*,' and in English, 'It is raining.' They all have a common meaning that the translator preserves while translating. It is a proposition that is primarily true or false. The object of a belief (or a desire or hope or fear) is a proposition, which is what *that* clause in the sentence 'I believe that the cat sat on the mat' refers to. Statements can be true or false, too, but they are secondary bearers of truth or falsity.
>
> **The Law of Non-Contradiction:** This is one of the laws of logic that states that it is impossible for a proposition and its negation (the symbol for negation is '~', which can be read as 'not') to be both true at the same time. Which translates into saying that (P & ~P) is always false ('&' is the symbol for 'and' (conjunction) in logic). For instance, it cannot be both true that Mewmew is a cat and it is not the case that Mewmew is a cat at the same time and is thus always false. It's just not possible for something to have incompatible properties at the same time. When two people contradict each other, one says P and the other says ~P. Both cannot be right at the same time.

statement shows that they're not really disagreeing like in the case of 'tasty'.

A major argument for relativism is that since there is no way to go beyond our limited cultural or individual perspectives to judge that a belief or statement is actually true, there is no such thing as absolute truth. Truths are only relative to an individual or culture. A person in the West cannot transcend their limited Western perspective and culturally developed standards to judge a non-Western perspective, for instance, on the efficacy of witchcraft to be false. The best explanation for this inability to judge is that there is no such thing as perspective independent truth.

One motivation that people have for relativism is that they think it benefits society to believe in relativism. This is because people have thought that their beliefs are absolute and they have tried to force those beliefs onto people. Wars have also happened because of religions thinking theirs is the one true religion or some political ideology thinking it is the one true ideology. But this worry about tolerance should not really lead to relativism because people can still be tolerant if they hold that 'tolerance is good' is absolutely true.

Relativism leads to massive problems.[v] A major problem is that if we take relativism seriously, there is no way our attempts to represent reality (which is what we aim for when we try to form a belief) succeed or fail. Take the belief of people in the twelfth century who held on to the geocentric model of the universe: The sun revolves around the earth. However, in the twelfth century, the sun did NOT revolve around the earth. Now a person who understands the word 'true' in English will accept this: 'If P, then it is *true* that P.' For instance, if snow is falling, then it is *true* that snow is falling. In the twelfth century, if the sun didn't revolve around the earth, then it is *true* that in the twelfth century, the sun didn't revolve around the earth. The belief of people in the twelfth century was mistaken precisely because it was *true* in the twelfth century that the sun didn't revolve around the earth. If the relativist is right, there's no way the belief of twelfth-century people can be false! Because as per the relativist, it isn't really true that the sun doesn't revolve around the earth but only true according to me.

Another objection to relativism is that it doesn't allow for the possibility of undiscovered truths. There are exact details of distant stars that we may never know. Let's take 'if P, then it is *true* that P' again. If there is limestone 2,500 feet beneath me, it is *true* that there is limestone 2,500 feet beneath me. That's why we can say that undiscovered truths exist. If the world is a certain way, it is *true* that the world is a certain way. But if truths are only true for someone, these undiscovered truths don't exist since even these facts don't exist independently of what people believe. It's only true according to them that these facts exist. Relativism thus denies that there is a difference between what is true (which can be independent of what is known, like undiscovered truths) and what is known to be true.

There are two replies the relativist can make here. One is to say that the absolutist about truth is assuming what they are trying to prove. For there to be undiscovered truths and to believe that the earth actually revolves around the sun instead of the truth of it depending on a culture, they have to assume that relativism is already mistaken.

A classic response to this is that if the relativist believes that her opponent is wrong, then the relativist believes the opponent is mistaken because 'all truths are relative' is absolutely true and not relatively true. As a result, relativism is self-defeating because it leads to the contradiction that all truth is relative and some truth is non-relative. The relativist might still reply that, okay, the opponent is not absolutely mistaken about only mistake according to the relativist. The problem again is that the relativist now holds that 'there is no such thing as being mistaken' to be true absolutely!

Here's another possible response by the relativist. A fact is merely something (a statement or a proposition) that is verified or proven. This is a common view of what a fact is. This is often contrasted with an opinion: An opinion is an expression of a thought, feeling or belief. The relativist may argue that since a fact is what is verified or proven, a fact depends on whether we prove or verify it. Therefore, there can be no unverified undiscovered facts.

This common distinction between fact and opinion is highly confused. It's confused because I might express my belief that the earth revolves around the sun, and it is verified and pretty certain (which is characteristic of a fact).[vi] So first, the fact-opinion distinction is a false dilemma. A false dilemma is an informal fallacy where we are asked to pick from two options when there are more options available. In this case, the exclusive choice between either fact or opinion is a false dilemma because the belief can be either true or false after verification and yet be a (so-called) fact. That's the third option.

Second, the above understanding of fact as a verified proposition makes the existence of facts depend on humans. This is precisely what is being questioned when it is argued that relativism doesn't allow for undiscovered facts. The relativist cannot merely reassert their argument that facts depend on humans because it is only true according to someone that facts exist *because* truth is relative. It's like when you argue against someone and they respond to your arguments by just repeating their argument or their claim. (Instead of using the fact–opinion distinction, one can just talk about propositions that are verified or proven and propositions that aren't.)

If relativism is right, then the only facts that exist are those that are known to be true. As a result, the existence of facts is relative to people. But if facts depend upon them being proven, then facts don't exist until proven. That's very strange because we discover facts like there being a particular sort of bacteria. We don't invent them, or they don't suddenly come into being

> **Metaphysics:** Metaphysics is the study of the nature of reality. For example, as we saw, Descartes' claim about the essence of the mind being thought and the essence of the body being matter was a metaphysical claim. We will also see that looking at the nature of free will and personal identity are metaphysical pursuits.

Ontology: Ontology is a branch of metaphysics that asks questions about what exists. Descartes' claim that the world has two types of things, mental and material, is an ontological claim. Questions about whether God exists or whether free will exists are ontological questions.

Epistemology: Epistemology is the theory of knowledge. It studies the nature and scope of knowledge, what we can know, whether we can know, the role of experience and reason in giving rise to knowledge and the methods of knowledge.

because they're proven.

What is happening in the above line of thinking is the confusion between an ontological point and an epistemological point. Whether we can know something is different from whether a thing exists. We might not know that something exists, but it is still possible for it to exist. We may never come to know how many steps the dinosaur whose fossil was discovered walked, but the fact would still have existed. We can see this confusion in the relativist's initial argument, too. From whether people can go beyond their perspective, which is an epistemological claim, the argument leaps to conclude something about whether the truth exists absolutely. People might not be able to know the truth through some perspective independent criteria, but truth will still exist.

If relativism completely holds ground in society, it's impossible to actually disagree about facts. People disagree when one says, 'The earth is spherical,' and another says, 'The earth is not spherical.' Disagreement (in this case) occurs when people pick out the same thing but disagree about what property it has. The people disagreeing hold that the earth exists and that the earth has a shape that doesn't depend on what anyone thinks or believes. With relativism on the prowl, we might even witness suspicion between people with differing views, who refuse to hear what the other person has to say. Each person thinks that the others' views are merely an expression of power, truth being merely a function of what power dictates.

Last but not the least, if relativism is true, then philosophical enquiry is futile. If the questions have no answers that are true but are only true for you and me, why should I look for answers?

Fortunately, one of the laws of logic is the law of excluded middle. It states that for any proposition, either that proposition or its negation obtains (obtains is just a fancy word for occurs or exists). This is symbolized as: for any P, P v ~P ('v' is the symbol for 'or' (disjunction) in logic). You can see why the law is true because of what 'not' means. If ~P obtains (like it is not snowing at this exact spot s), then this excludes every case where P obtains (it is snowing at this exact spot s) and includes every other case (it might be raining at that spot, not raining and not snowing, hailing, sunny, etc.). If P occurs, then ~P doesn't occur and vice versa. There can't be a situation where neither P nor ~P occurs. That is impossible.[vii]

So for a philosophical question like whether free will exists, either free will exists or it is not the case that free will exists. There has to be an answer. We might never know the answer, but there is one. No harm in trying to look for answers to philosophical questions then. Let's begin.

THE MEANING OF LIFE

Absurdity and the Meaning of Life

Sisyphus was a character in Greek mythology and the king of Corinth. Zeus, the chief god, had kidnapped the river god Asopus's daughter by taking the form of a bird, and Sisyphus had told Asopus which way Zeus had carried her. Angry that his secret had been revealed, Zeus sent Thanatos (Death) to tie Sisyphus in chains in the underworld. A crafty Sisyphus tricked Death, put him in chains instead and escaped. Since people couldn't die and battles weren't fun any more, Ares, god of war, freed Death. But before Sisyphus was sent back to the underworld, he told his wife, Merope, to not bury him and stop making traditional sacrifices after he died. Once in the underworld, Hades sent Sisyphus back to the land of the living to punish Merope. His zest for life was such that he tricked the gods a second time, and this time, he lived a complete life. For his crime against the gods, he is punished for an eternity of rolling up a huge boulder up a hill, which rolls back when it's about to reach the top. And so, Sisyphus has the pointless task of rolling the boulder up again and again forever and ever.

Albert Camus, in his essay 'The Myth of Sisyphus',[i] uses this myth to illustrate the sense of the absurd when it comes to our lives. The way Sisyphus's task is pointless and without a goal, we, too, can have a sense that life is that way. Camus gives the reason for the feeling of absurdity by wondering what makes a person commit suicide. Life being difficult, people still go on living, a major reason being habit. But what makes a person choose suicide is to see that given that there is no reason to explain the purpose of the world and life, this habit of life is ridiculous and the suffering is pointless.

This is symptomatic of the human situation, where it looks like a universe that was once full of purpose, order and meaning no longer has all these. Nature, which was once full of beauty and where the sky felt soft and the pattern of trees felt clear and meaningful, doesn't have this illusion of meaning, unity and pattern any more. The world that was familiar to us seems unfamiliar, what felt like home doesn't feel like it. It instead feels hostile because we can't attribute meaning and purpose to it. We had anthropomorphized it, that is, thought of it as having human traits. But the scientific and mechanistic view of the world, in which events in nature occur blindly and atoms are mere atoms, makes the world to us what it always was – bereft of purpose, particularly divine purpose. As William Wordsworth put it in his 'Ode: Intimations of Immortality from Recollections of Early Childhood':

> There was a time when meadow, grove, and stream,
>
> The earth, and every common sight,
> To me did seem
> Apparelled in celestial light,
> The glory and the freshness of a dream.
> It is not now as it hath been of yore;—
> Turn wheresoe'er I may,
> By night or day.
> The things which I have seen I now can see no more.[ii]

This tension between the human desire for clarity and purpose versus blind nature in the face of an unintelligible and indifferent universe is what, for Camus, gives rise to the feeling of the absurd. You can see a similar conflict between Sisyphus's passion for life and the purposelessness of the task in his punishment. For Sisyphus, that would have led to a feeling of absurdity.

Now Camus imagines Sisyphus walking back from the summit after the boulder has started rolling back down. On the way back, not only is he is reminded of his suffering, but he's also conscious of it. It is Sisyphus's awareness and clarity about his suffering, as well as his defiance of it, that makes him transcend his fate. The acknowledgement of the truth of his fate makes his go beyond it. It's like when one listens to sad, beautiful music, the melancholy disappears. For Sisyphus, in acknowledging his fate and carrying on in his struggle by defying it, he becomes its master and can carry on back to the boulder in this silent joy. Camus thus says, 'The struggle itself towards the heights is enough to fill a man's heart. One must imagine Sisyphus happy.' For us, too, we can live on defying an indifferent universe, acknowledge the absurdity and being ennobled by this and carry on with the struggle of our existence.

Richard Taylor on the Meaning of Life

Richard Taylor, in his essay 'The Meaning of Human Existence',[iii] first looks at the image of a meaningless life to figure out what's missing in it to think about what leads to a meaningful life. For him, the meaninglessness of Sisyphus's task doesn't lie in his immense toil in rolling the boulder because a lot of meaningful tasks also need a lot of toil. The reason his task is meaningless is because it is endlessly repetitive and doesn't really have a purpose. It is pointless because there's no significant outcome and just the same thing again and again. And it would still be pointless if the boulder hadn't been frustratingly rolling back but he was stacking one boulder on top of another.

When it comes to the pointlessness of non-human animal life,

Taylor gives the example of a ground mole. The animal has vestigial eyes that can only tell light from darkness. Throughout its life, all it does is struggle to survive by getting from one place to another with a lot of effort and finally eating a worm or something to nourish it. And then it regains energy for another hunt and so on. Then it reproduces, and this cycle will rinse and repeat, just like Sisyphus. And this sort of endless repetitive and meaningless cycle is the case with the entire animal kingdom. Taylor extends this picture of a meaningless existence to humans, too, who get up every day and repeat the same patterns of life where they do more or less what they did the previous day, even if they find a few satisfactions and moments of happiness. Then they leave the world with not much of a difference with another generation to perpetuate the same cycle. This is like Macbeth's speech in Shakespeare's play:

> Tomorrow, and tomorrow, and tomorrow,
> Creeps in this petty pace from day to day,
> To the last syllable of recorded time;
> And all our yesterdays have lighted fools
> The way to dusty death. Out, out, brief candle!
> Life's but a walking shadow, a poor player,
> That struts and frets his hour upon the stage,
> And then is heard no more. It is a tale
> Told by an idiot, full of sound and fury,
> Signifying nothing.[iv]

But one may respond, what if one is filled with a zeal for life, despite it being repetitive, and finds pleasure and satisfaction in it? Taylor asks us to imagine the gods implanting an intense desire to do what he does, and as a result, he ends up enjoying it and finds the fulfilment of his desire. Sisyphus finding fulfilment in what he does doesn't make it less meaningless. So, even though we can end up enjoying our endlessly repetitive lives, our lives are still without meaning.

Since he's looked at repetitiveness and pointlessness as leading to a meaningless life, Taylor tries to come up with a positive account for a meaningful life.

Now suppose Sisyphus was not only piling rock upon rock, but the rocks also went on to build a magnificent and beautiful temple, as beautiful as the Taj Mahal. At least we can now say that what he does has some meaning, given that there's some result. But suppose he will eternally keep adding to it but that work of the temple will never ever be completed. So one ingredient to a meaningful life Taylor comes up with is that it should be at least possible to attain one's goals and not merely pursue them. This seems to run contrary to Camus' view above, according to which Sisyphus can only go against his absurdity by means of his struggle.

However, being able to complete the temple isn't sufficient to make a life meaningful because Sisyphus might have still been a slave under someone else's control. It might be that he understands why he's doing what he's doing, but it's still the case that his ultimate goal is not his. He is subject to someone else's will, and he's merely an instrument in its fulfilment. Another ingredient then, that Taylor adds to a meaningful like, is that one's goals should be one's own creation and choice rather than imposed on one.

Further, think of Sisyphus as not being punished but rolling these stones as per the plan of his own creative mind. He sets out to create this temple that will be a lasting thing of beauty to himself, gods and mortals. Taylor thus lays out all the ingredients of a life that is meaningful: The life has to have a purpose but not just any purpose that satisfies since one can live one's entire life just digging the deepest hole ever and be satisfied, but that's not meaningful. The purpose has to be a noble and good one, like Sisyphus's temple. For a meaningful life, the goal should be achievable and lasting. And finally, the purpose should be one's own and be creative.

For Taylor, the most meaningful lives are not led by military strategists or wealth builders but by poets, philosophers, writers and composers. And creativity doesn't merely involve creating an object but also looking at the world in creative ways, like looking at a flower creatively and finding it beautiful. Creativity need not mean you become a great poet since even ordinary thoughts can be poetic. Someone can even be creative in their relationships, thoughts and emotions. People of genius are more likely to lead lives of such creativity, but we can, too.

While Taylor seems to be on the right track, it seems to overgeneralize the repetitiveness of our lives, and by doing so, almost removes the meaningfulness we actually find in it. It's like he takes a bird's eye view and can't see things that are actual. Perhaps there are more things to life than he says that make it meaningful. Doing something noble and good sounds right, but it is possible that people who aren't that creative can live very meaningful lives, too. For instance, a soldier doing marching drills and generally following orders. We'll look at this further in the sections below.

Nagel on Absurdity and Meaning

Unlike Camus, the philosopher Thomas Nagel, who is still alive and a professor of philosophy at New York University, has a different notion of what leads to the feeling of the absurd, and thus, a different idea about how we can live on despite it. Nagel[v] says that the absurd arises as a result of a mismatch between aspiration and reality. In everyday life, Nagel gives examples of a person's pants falling off while being knighted and an infamous criminal becoming the head of a big philanthropic foundation. But when it comes to life as a whole, the absurd arises due to a clash between the serious attitude that we have towards life, our plans and projects on one hand and the possibility of whatever we take as serious being arbitrary and its value being doubted.

Our ability to find the absurd arises because we possess self-consciousness, due to which we can reflect on the consequences of our decisions and activities and whether they are worth it. That's how we can detach ourselves and ask the *why* question about the lives we lead. The perspective we have when we actually live our lives is what Nagel calls the subjective perspective, and the one that occurs as a result of detachment and abstraction from it is the objective perspective.

When we look at life from the objective perspective, it looks like we take the reasons for which we do things for granted, and we don't know how to defend them. When I start asking why I do this or that, it looks like for everything, there's no reason why I did this rather than that, and it all looks arbitrary and insignificant. Of course, we might be able to give an immediate reason, but it looks like even that reason can be called into question, and so on. The absurd, for Nagel, arises because we can take this external detached view of ourselves and yet lead our lives.

Recall that for Camus, the absurd came about because of the clash between our desire for meaning and order and the world lacking that due to being blind and indifferent. Nagel argues against this – that even if the world had a God-given purpose, we could still question that purpose and have doubts about it. For instance, in the face of intense suffering and misfortune, I can still question and doubt God's purpose in the world. For Nagel, the absurd would still arise since that is a mismatch between aspiration and reality and because we can doubt this due to the objective perspective.

On how we ought to lead our lives in the face of the absurd, Nagel finds Camus' idea that we should face a blind and indifferent world with defiance to be unnecessarily grandiose, dramatic and self-pitying. He says that absurdity doesn't require us to be disturbed the way Camus is. Absurdity is merely a result of the human capacity to take a step back and possess an objective perspective. Instead of despair or dramatic heroism, we return to leading a normal life after having doubted its seriousness. But once we return, we can't see life the same way again. We can take a serious attitude towards our lives, but that is tinged with a sense of irony. We might not have the reasons for our projects and lives, but we still go on due to something deeper. If there is no reason to see why anything in life matters, then even that doesn't matter, and so we lead our lives with a sense of irony.

There is a problem, however, with Camus, Taylor and Nagel's views of the absurd. Susan Wolf[vi] argues against this that it's not obvious that we would have the expectation that the cosmos is full of significance and meaning. In fact, we tend to carry on with our projects without this grandiose delusion that what we do is cosmically significant. The mother sacrificing her sleep to care for her sick baby or the Olympic athlete who takes pains to better herself to break a world record hardly seems to be thinking about its significance to the universe.

Meaning in Life

The philosophers we have encountered till now have been asking the question: What is the meaning of life? Camus and Nagel have been looking for the ultimate or cosmic meaning of life. Their response is that since life and the world don't originate with the divine and lack a purpose given by God or gods, they have no significance. But as we saw, most people don't have such grand expectations. Even if there is no meaning in life, a purpose that's externally given by God or gods, we can still find meaning. So how do we find meaning in life?

Hedonism

Hedonists hold that what ultimately matters in life is happiness and that happiness is the same as pleasure. Everything we do is valuable and significant so long as it leads to pleasure. Suppose we ask why we do something, say, why do I work, and one answer would be to earn money, and if we follow the chain of whys, we'll answer we do all this for happiness. For Epicureans, happiness is pleasure. Hedonists also hold that something is bad if it leads to pain.

Epicurus (341–270 BCE), from whose name we get the word 'epicureanism', was a major proponent of this view. Epicurus argues in his *Letter to Menoeceus*[vii] that our final goal is freedom from pain and fear, and everything we prefer or avoid is to ensure that the body is healthy and the mind tranquil. He counts the final goal of freedom from fear and pain to be a sort of pleasure. Once we have attained this, then we don't look around for something else that is lacking, and this is thus the final end (goal) of everything we do.

This doesn't mean that we go after everything that gives pleasure since the result of a pleasure can be an even bigger discomfort. And we don't always avoid pain at all costs since facing some pains can result in a bigger pleasure than we would've had if we had avoided the pain. The view also doesn't mean that one is devoted to sensual pleasures like going on non-stop binge sex or drinking for days. He advises that one can be content with little, simple pleasures if one isn't very well off, and even a simple meal can be as pleasurable as a costly one. Epicurus also says, 'It is sober reasoning, searching out the grounds of every choice and avoidance, and banishing those beliefs through which the greatest disturbances take possession of the soul.'

For hedonists then, pleasure becomes a standard by which to judge the worth of all actions. This means while pleasure is a direct value, everything else has a value that is only indirect. For instance, you use your pen to write, so your pen is valuable in this context only to write. But what it means for pleasure to have direct value is that it is valuable for its own sake. You play cricket for pleasure's sake, but you don't have pleasure for something else's sake – it's valuable for its own sake. That's how pleasure becomes the standard – since everything you do has indirect value in relation to it, it is valuable.

Pain also has direct value. It's directly bad since it's absurd to ask why your pain is bad if you get hit on the knee with a cricket bat. Thus, something is bad if it leads to pain, and so pain is also a standard to judge. Note that pleasure can have direct and indirect value, too. You have pleasure at having solved a maths problem which leads you to solve more math problems, and then you get great marks at the exam and have pleasure at the end of it.

As good and commonsensical as hedonism sounds, it is seriously flawed. For hedonism, pleasure is valued not because it facilitates us to do something else but because of the quality of the inner feeling itself. The philosopher Robert Nozick[viii] argues that we care about other things apart from merely the felt quality of our experiences, so pleasure is not what ultimately matters. He imagines a thought experiment to go against hedonism. Imagine that there is an experience machine which, if you are plugged into, you can experience anything you want. You can write amazing poems, love the one you desire, etc. What's more, once plugged, you'll forget that your experiences have been generated by the machine so that knowledge doesn't spoil your pleasures. The question he raises then is: Would you choose to plug into this machine for whatever is left of your life?

For most people, the answer would be no. Even those who would initially say yes would realize that they overcame their initial reservations against being plugged into the machine. What's the lesson from this? Suppose a person thinks they're very accomplished artistically, but people just fake it when they appear to like their work. Another person is really happy because of what seems to be a successful marriage, but his partner keeps cheating behind their back. We pity these people because their pleasure is based on things that aren't the case, that don't exist. This is why we don't want to be plugged into the experience machine. We want to feel pleasure because what matters to us is more than inner felt experience. What matters is that the situations we are happy about actually occur; otherwise, we're deluded. What is valuable to us is that we are connected to reality so we can explore and act upon it, change and create new things in it.

We're also alone in the experience machine and disconnected from other people. So what we care about is also sharing a reality with other people. Nozick also says that we don't want happy moments all the time (that'll be tiresome!). We care about other feelings, too, as part of being human, of understanding the world around us, of connecting to people in a deep manner, of the profound feelings arising out of music and tragedy and doing creative and original stuff. People care about the kind of life to which happiness is an appropriate response and to have that response in the light of that life.

Atheistic Existentialism

Jean-Paul Sartre was a very famous French philosopher, playwright and novelist. For him, we don't discover values, meaning and purpose but invent them. What does this mean, and what is his argument for such a conclusion?

Sartre's[ix] atheistic existentialism has a core claim: 'existence precedes essence'. Typically, by essence, philosophers mean the nature of a thing, that is, the properties that make a thing what it is, like H_2O is the essence of water. Sartre's example is that an artefact like a paper cutter. The artisan creates it with a concept in mind, which includes the procedure with which it is to be made and what it's used for. That's the essence. When the artisan creates the paper cutter, the essence in the mind of the artisan comes first and the paper cutter comes into existence later. In this case, the essence precedes the existence.

If God is thought to be an artisan, then if God exists, he will have the essence (the techniques with which he creates them and purpose) of humans before in his head and the existence of humans will come later. But if God doesn't exist, then there is no essence that God can conceive of before. Humans thus have no predefined nature and purpose. They first merely exist, then propel themselves into the future and define themselves. 'Man is nothing else but what he makes of himself,' says Sartre. In the end, since values can't be found outside of humans like in God, humans have to invent value.

Sartre illustrates how you have to invent value by means of the example of his student who comes to him for advice. The student's father was in conflict with his mother and wanted to be a collaborator with the Germans, who were enemies of the French during World War II (Sartre and the student were French). The older brother was killed by Germans. The student had to choose between avenging his brother by going off to England to join the Free French Forces and staying with his mother and caring for her since he was all she had. Going to England would crush her. So he had to make a decision between another individual and the collective. In the end, he himself has to decide, since any priest he goes to has to be his own decision and the priest's advice might be based on loyalties to the Germans or the French. If that is so, then the student already knows the answer the priest is going to give. Which means that his decision on the answer has already been made by him by choosing to go to which priest. He also knows the answer Sartre would give him, which is, 'You're free to choose, that is, invent.'

He can't look to an ethical code either since the Christian one says love your neighbour and so on, but that can't help him decide whom he should love more, his fighting comrades or his mother. Suppose he goes with Kant's dictum, 'Never treat any person as a means, but as an end,' which means basically don't use people for your convenience. If he stays with his mom and treats her as an end, he'll treat those fighting as a means (so he gets the security to be with his mom), but if he treats those fighting as an end, then he might treat his mom as a means.

In the end, then, everyone is forlorn, which means they have to freely choose the way they are and live. You have to freely invent value. For Sartre, if you delude yourself into thinking you aren't free to make your decision, then you're acting in bad faith, like a waiter who thinks he must identify with his social role and has no other choice than to have the mannerisms he has as the waiter, wake up at 5 a.m., etc. It's like you think that essence, that is, your social role, precedes your existence, that you are like a rock or a cauliflower. Thus, only because value is chosen by free agents can things have value.

But one can immediately see problems with Sartre's view. One objection to Sartre is that if you stub your toe, you don't invent the value of pain, that it is bad, but you discover it.[x] Another objection given by Susan Wolf[xi] to a theory like Sartre's is that suppose someone freely decides to keep writing copies of *War and Peace* by hand for the rest of their lives or keep playing Sudoku, then it looks like they're not inventing value in these cases at least since these projects aren't worthwhile.

Susan Wolf on the Meaning of Life

In recent times, the philosopher Susan Wolf is one of the foremost contributors to the meaning of life. She says that 'meaningful lives are lives of active engagement in projects of worth'.[xii] She understands 'active engagement' with something or someone about which and whom we are passionate about. When we are actively engaged, we feel alive and involved, caught up in the experience and excited. Climbing a mountain, caring for a sick friend and writing a book can involve stress, sadness and danger, so active engagement isn't necessarily a pleasant experience. Active engagement is important for a meaningful life because people can be bored or alienated, even if they are good with what they do, like a doctor or a housewife and mother. Their utter lack of being engaged with their actions can make their lives seem meaningless to them.

But for Wolf, active engagement isn't a sufficient condition for a meaningful life. Consider the case of Sisyphus again as we saw from Taylor, with the gods implanting him with an intense urge to keep doing what he does. This isn't meaningful, even though he finds satisfaction in what he's doing. Wolf gives the case of people who are overcome with a single passion in life to collect rubber bands or count how many tiles there are on the bathroom floor and counting them again and again all their lives. Doing worthless things can make one's life meaningless.

Wolf gives a more general meaning to 'projects' than just projects, like mastering a subject, finding a cure for cancer or building a house, which do add meaning to life. But she also means relationships and involvements with friends, family, communities and even planning a surprise party for one's partner. She also includes the kinds of interaction with worthwhile things that give rise to meaning like 'creating, promoting, protecting (worthwhile) things, from helping people one loves and people in need, from achieving levels of skill and excellence, from overcoming obstacles, from gaining understanding, and even from just communing with or actively appreciating what is there to be appreciated'.[xiii]

Let's look at a few objections to this account since this is one of the big ones currently out there. One major objection is that what she is saying is elitist, and since we can be wrong about what really counts as worthwhile, who's to say what is worthwhile? People have been wrong throughout when some geniuses and explorers' activities weren't seen as having value and were thus mocked. People also overrate activities. Wolf's response to this is that we can in open-minded ways and through community deliberate and come to conclusions about the value and worth of something. As we do that, the process of reasoning would help us come up with standards for judging what is worthwhile and what is not.

For instance, the process of reasoning can be something like this. Suppose I find philosophy to be worthless because it's too abstract and unconnected with everyday life. But I still read some of it here and there, and the puzzles and problems seem like fun but still worthless. I keep reading more and more and realize that I am good at it and can come up with original arguments. I find that I have become increasingly clear in my thinking, can clarify conceptual confusion in many areas of life, my comprehension of everything else including philosophy improves, I can imagine thought experiments that fire up my imagination, and I can look at things and think and reason about them in a very different way from other people. As I master the subject, it becomes more meaningful to me, even more so since it allows me to look beyond myself, my desires and society's desires, which are limited to the immediate context. I realize that it's not useless because, as has been in history, philosophy didn't seem relevant at the current moment, but the sciences, computer science and movements in the arts and architecture came out of it. So I don't know what will come of it but having a storehouse of knowledge not immediately relevant might be helpful for us humans. It also seems valuable since, as rational beings, it is up to us to resolve contradictions that we seemingly believe in, and philosophy helps do that.

As for the charge of elitism, Wolf's answer is that finding some projects valuable and having a hierarchy doesn't automatically give us license to judge people's lives since we may be wrong about the things we estimate to be meaningful.

Flow and the Meaning of Life

A major worry that Wolf's account faces is that projects of worth need to have values as objective. This is very odd since, if they are objective and not subjective and they're not found in a world full of atoms and particles described by physics, then where are they? They might be in a heaven outside space and time (called a Platonic heaven since Plato was famous for the idea of this nonspatiotemporal heaven). This is very odd since one worry is if they are separate from us, and causality can only occur within space and time, how can we know then since we're not related to them in any chain of cause and effect (which we are when we know about the things around us).

The psychologist Jonathan Haidt helps Wolf by saying that she really doesn't need value to be objective for her account to work.[xiv] Wolf's fear is that if she denies objective value, then things like lawn-mower racing and sitting on flagpoles for long periods of time will be as meaningful as composing a symphony. Haidt says that Wolf's active engagement is like the psychologist Mihály Csíkszentmihályi's concept of vital engagement. Vital engagement is defined as 'a relationship to the world that is characterized both by experiences of flow (enjoyed absorption) and by meaning (subjective significance)'.[xv] Flow is basically being in the zone and occurs when one is completely absorbed in a challenging task that one is skilled in. So your attention is fully focused, and even though your self is involved, you lose consciousness of it. Flow is in contrast to bodily pleasures like sex and food, which can lead to disgust if one indulges in excess.

Flow can be achieved in creative activities like painting and writing, in music while singing or with a skilled person playing the piano, physical activities like sports and driving on winding roads and even an intense conversation. While playing tennis, each stroke can bring flashes of positive feelings, like each brushstroke made in a painting. Flow itself is a deep interest and not meaning as such, but people begin a lot of activities they go on to master with a deep interest, which gives them glimpses of flow. As people create more knowledge, identity, relationships, action around that activity over the years, vital engagement emerges. Think about what I said about my experience with philosophy. It looks like my initial deep interest led to vital engagement over the years as I mastered the subject.

Now Haidt says that less meaningful activities like lawn-mower racing and flagpole sitting are fun, but they aren't very meaningful because there's no flow. Activities that we eventually develop flow in are ones that we are intensely curious about and gain knowledge of and order our lives so we can pursue them.

Observe that in the case of flow, meaning isn't objective in the sense that is mind-independent, but it's objective in the sense that their occurrence isn't dependent upon our beliefs as such (we might believe that meaningless activities will lead to flow, but they don't) but upon how we are biologically and the ways in which we interact with the world.

The Bhagavadgita and the Meaning of Life

The Bhagavadgita is a section of the epic Mahabharata right before the war between two sides who are cousins, the Pandavas and the Kauravas, and their armies. Arjuna, the general, asks his charioteer, the god Krishna, to go to the middle of the battlefield so he can survey the men in the battlefield. Arjuna is moved by compassion and despair when he see his own kin and teachers. He is torn between his duty to his family and his duty towards his caste, the kshatriya warrior caste. In the modern context, think of the duty towards one's caste as the duty you have in your roles in life in your family, your profession, society, and so on. Note, this dilemma isn't just one between a moral and an immoral choice but between two choices that have values that are compelling.[xvi] Lord Krishna's response to him shows the path he must take.

Krishna's first reply to Arjuna is to tell him to focus on the permanent, which is the universe and the values in it, not on what changes and is temporary (we've seen the scientific picture implying no values in the universe, but more on that later). If Arjuna fights, he acts according to those permanent values of his duty as a warrior. Lord Krishna talks about reincarnation and how everyone on the battlefield has always existed and will do so even after death, when the person will live in another body. He tells Arjuna to bear pain or pleasure, cold and heat that arise from experiences with patience since they are fleeting.

He thus says, 'The impermanent has no reality; reality lies in the eternal... Realize that which pervades the universe and is indestructible; no power can affect this unchanging, imperishable reality. The body is mortal, but that which dwells in the body is immortal and immeasurable. Therefore, Arjuna, fight in this battle.' (Bhagavadgita 2:16–18)[xvii]

What one is devoted to making meaningful choices is 'skill in action', which is yoga.[xviii] Now this yoga is translated as discipline and is not yoga in the physical and spiritual exercises that are popular today. This discipline is what enables us to perform and succeed in our actions.

Krishna elaborates on three kinds of discipline. *Karma* yoga, which is the yoga of action, *jnana* yoga, the yoga of knowledge, and *bhakti* yoga, the yoga of devotion.

The discipline of *Karma* yoga is to act in a way without regard for one's own benefit and the result of one's actions but in a spirit of sacrifice for others.[xix] For your choice to be meaningful, you can't be attached to the results of action, specifically selfish and ego-oriented results. That is, you shouldn't be performing the action because you're going to get a reward. Indifference or non-attachment to the results isn't the same as not having any feeling or concern whatsoever. It simply means being unbiased and uninfluenced by selfish desire in one's actions based on knowledge of how the world actually is.[xx] The goal of all actions is the cohesion of the whole, that is, to increase cooperation and mutual interdependence in the world, which includes the social, moral and cosmic worlds.[xxi]

The reason Krishna says this is because obsessing about the results can make you anxious and miserable. But more importantly, you can control your actions, but you can't control the results. It's also important to not be attached to the objects that are given by the senses because attachment to them increases the lust to possess them, which gives rise to anger. You can't learn from your mistakes because anger messes with your judgement. And if you can't make correct choices, your life turns into a mess. The discipline gives you freedom and self-control from your own impulses to act. Action is also seen as a sacrifice, like a sacrificial offering to the gods. So action becomes a ritual. This looks like action is given a sense of the sacred and thus gets saturated with significance and meaning. Rituals also structure and give pattern and order to our lives and make them less chaotic. We mark the significance of an event through a ritual and include it in the narrative of our lives and society, an event that otherwise would have just passed us by. It looks like all actions done as rituals would do the same.

The discipline of knowledge, *jnana* yoga, is to act with the knowledge of one's true permanent self which is one with the cosmos. The discipline involves being able to discriminate between the reality of fleeting appearances and permanent reality. This allows one to understand what's temporary and permanent and act in the light of the permanent. Knowledge enables us to act without being pulled by selfish and short-lived desires. Arjuna does wonder why, if knowledge is superior to action, he has to fight the war. Krishna replies that without action, no one can exist. Action is better than inaction since action is required even to sustain the body.

Last but not the least, Krishna talks of the discipline of *bhakti* (devotion), where one surrenders oneself to Krishna, the object of devotion.

> Fill your mind with me; love me; serve me; worship me always. Seeking me in your heart, you will at last be united with me. – (Bhagavadgita 9:34)

Think about this. It might seem that we're losing out a lot on our passions in *Karma* yoga. But it is the passion of devotion that seems to be compensating for this and seems to be the cause of motivations. One can think of devotion to Krishna, even if one doesn't believe in Krishna or God as a metaphor for one's devotion and loyalty to goals that are more than ego-centric goals.

Notice that the discipline of *Karma* yoga sounds like the sort of skill-based actions that might involve flow. Not only do your actions involve skill (yoga as 'skill in action'), they also need to have full focus that is under the control of the will since one isn't distracted by desires.[xxii]

The philosopher Julia Annas argues for the exercise of virtues that Aristotle talks about, like being just and courage and others, that they involve flow. For Aristotle, a virtue is the excellence of a person like the excellence of a knife is that it cuts well. It's a character trait that can be evidenced in one's actions because it's been built through habit. Aristotle compares virtue, which involves a skill, to practical skills:

> For the things we have to learn before we can do them, we learn by doing them, e.g. men become builders by building and lyre-players by playing the lyre; so too we become just by doing just acts, temperate by doing temperate acts, brave by doing brave acts.[xxiii]

Annas talks about virtue involving flow, where the flow experience is rewarding for its own sake, even if the activity is done for another goal. She gives the example of a person throwing a ball through a hoop in basketball, where the attempt itself is enjoyable whether the hoop passes through or not. This might be the experience of the person exercising *Karma* yoga, where there is no attachment to the reward. Similarly, flow involves a loss of self-consciousness, and this sounds very much like *Karma* yoga, where one acts not for one's egotistical desires. Perhaps the practice was seen the way it was because of the loss of consciousness of the self.

Jnana and *bhakti* yoga, too, have insights into the meaning of life in a modern context. Another objection to Susan Wolf that Haidt raises is that her view is too atomistic and focused on the individual. Haidt points out Wolf as saying:

> I am *drawn* by the particular values of my friend, of philosophy, of a great chocolate cake. These are "*objects*" whose value has a source outside myself. They would be good, or interesting, or worthwhile whether I liked or cared about or even noticed them or not. But they are values I *respond* to, for which I have an *affinity*... (emphasis added)[xxiv]

For Haidt, it's better to assume that the group is the basic unit of society rather than the individual. In fact, thinking that the individual is the basic unit is a recent Western idea from the seventeenth and eighteenth centuries. Under this conception, people are more self-conscious, prone to depression and wonder about the meaning of life.

The key, however, lies in the social nature of humans, which he compares to bees and chimps. Bees are ultrasocial, where the hive is a superorganism and individual bees are like cells in a body, willing to die for the group. Chimps, on the other hand, are moderately social and live in small groups, neither sacrificing their lives nor even sharing their food. Humans are more ultrasocial, 90 per cent chimp, 10 per cent bee.[xxv] We live in larger groups and exhibit team and tribal formation with a division of labour with practices, ideas and values that bind each other like a hive. He gives the example from Barbara Ehrenreich's *Dancing in the Streets: A History of Collective Joy*, which describes collective ecstatic dance as almost universal across cultures but to which Europeans responded with disgust. What the dance does is bind the group through love and weakens hierarchy. In fact, the historian William McNeill's book, which inspired Ehrenreich's book, describes the historian finding joy in synchronous drilling in the army. It became a sort of mystical experience to him, despite him finding it meaningless at first. This goes against Richard Taylor's view of creativity and one's purpose being essential to a meaningful life. The soldier follows orders and still has his experience to be meaningful. Haidt also mentions that collective practices, values and ideas are found sacred by groups that bind them when the hive mind is switched on.[xxvi] In fact, the hive mind is switched on even at the experience of awe at nature, where the ego gets dissolved and one feels that one is part of a whole.[xxvii]

Again, one may not believe in the existence of Krishna or that Krishna is one with the cosmos or God, or the nature of a permanent self that transcends time. But groups and their legacies are still more relatively permanent compared to the individual. This doesn't mean that one doesn't think of the individual at all since humans are still not fully bees. So we can think of the long-term effects of decisions, too, that may affect us. Even the Bible says, 'But seek ye first the kingdom of God, and his righteousness; and all these things shall be added unto you.' (Matthew 6:33)[xxviii] We can simply take this as a metaphor for thinking of the permanent, and that is what we're committed to.

Again, think of *jnana* yoga as knowledge of this permanent whole through the light of which we fulfil our roles to family, our jobs and society to perpetuate society and increase co-operation and value in it. And think of *bhakti* yoga involving devotion to that which is literally larger than ourselves, including the beauty of the cosmos, which might still be indifferent to us.

MORALITY

It looks pretty evident that committing an act of rape is morally wrong. And so was the Nazis killing Jews in concentration camps. Normative ethics is the area of philosophy that asks what makes actions like these morally wrong and what makes an action morally good.

But before we go to normative ethics, I want to clear up some preliminary confusions that a lot of people express, especially trendy undergrads and a whole lot of people in academia.

Cultural Relativism

The first confusion is the claim that morality is relative to a culture, that is, it varies across cultures and there's no absolute and universal moral norm.

The anthropologist Ruth Benedict writes about a North American Tribe called the Kwakiutl who saw the death of a person as an insult.[i] Whether it was from disease or being killed by an enemy didn't matter. The insult then had to be avenged by killing another person. In one instance, the sister and daughter of a chief go to a nearby town and don't return. The cause of death might have been bad whisky or a boat sinking. The chief then tells his warriors, 'Now I ask you tribes, who shall wail? Shall I do it, or shall another?' The spokesman replied, 'Not you Chief. Let some of the other tribes.'[ii] Setting up a war pole to declare their intent of returning the insult, they went and randomly killed seven men and two children who were sleeping. On returning home, they were left feeling good. And the victim's family don't hold anyone responsible for the death.

So says Benedict, these people would be seen as abnormal in our culture, and we would be seen abnormal in theirs. What is normal is defined by one's culture, and as societies go forward in history, they approve of some behaviours and disapprove of others. Morality is just those habits that have been approved by society, and what is morally good is just what has been a habit. This is just like how our language gets standardized, as well as our customs, such as dress. Since we are conditioned by these, we can't go outside what we are conditioned by to judge another culture's habits, since we'll be invariably judging them based on our upbringing.

Cultural relativism (CR) then says that 'x is good' means that 'the majority of a particular society approves of x'.[iii] Hitler was wrong merely means that he was wrong as per my society's standards. This is in contrast to saying that 'Hitler was wrong' absolutely, which is objective. One of the motivations for cultural relativism is that one should be more tolerant of other cultures; and as we saw, given that we are conditioned by our own societies, we'll inevitably be judging them through our lens. There's no way to escape our lens and we can't understand that culture well enough to judge it. Therefore, we shouldn't judge it.

The philosopher Bernard Williams[iv] points out a simple flaw with the argument. From the premise that 'right' means 'right for a given society' and 'wrong' means 'wrong for a given society', you can't conclude that it's wrong to judge (or condemn) a value in another society. Because the premise uses 'wrong' and 'right' in sense that is relative but the conclusion uses it in the non-relative sense. For the argument to be valid, they have to have the same sense, otherwise it's playing with an ambiguity.

Mary Midgley[v] also looks at the issue of judging other cultures, and wonders if it's not okay for us, or Westerners to criticize other cultural values, then it's not okay for people from other cultures to criticize ours or Western values. And yet anthropologists seem to be okay with the latter. She gives the example of a South American Indian who criticizes the way white Brazilians live and the anthropologist remarks that it was 'a damning indictment of Western civilization'. Of course, this isn't a knockdown argument, since someone can say that others can't criticize also, so Midgley goes further.

Judging can go both ways: praise and condemning. But Midgley asks, if we can't understand enough to criticize, we can't understand enough to praise another culture either. But we can and do praise other cultures, and if we praise blindly without understanding what we are praising, then our praise has no value. And we can still praise some things which we don't understand completely. For instance, when we want to learn from a stranger, we say 'there's something good here, but I can't make out what it is yet'. We can also distinguish people who are good enough for us to learn from and those who aren't.

The strange thing about cultural relativism would be that aspects of our own culture might be alien to us because we don't understand them and we have been conditioned by different values. Does that mean we can't judge it? Midgley asks us to consider how judgements work. We make judgements like *this is better* and *this is worse* so we must tacitly be appealing to some standard. Without some standard to judge against, we wouldn't have any opportunity to compare different people and learn from their wisdom or errors. This would apply to our own culture too.

This brings me to another major objection that's laid out in the literature. If we do hold the view that something is good because it is socially approved, I can't disagree with the values of my society, and the people who fought against racism or slavery or Jews being persecuted by Nazis would never have been able to disagree with the prevailing views. Why? Because disagreement involves saying something is 'socially approved' but that it isn't good. Accepting cultural relativism would remove agency from a person oppressed in their society or the person in the minority who disagrees with the majority view.

In fact, cultural relativism leads to a place where if the society approves of intolerance or cultural imperialism, this would be unobjectionable as any perspective.[vi] So either one accepts this or rejects cultural relativism. Cultural relativism immunizes any norms from the possibility of being wrong, even if they come about to ignorance because they are good as long as they are socially approved.

Psychological Egoism

Let's look at another common view about morality that's really confused.

One common theory about human psychology is called psychological egoism. This is the view that the only thing that we ultimately pursue is our own self-interest and that's all we are capable of desiring. This entails that any action we do is selfish, including moral actions which may seem unselfish but which we're ultimately doing for our happiness. This theory undermines a lot of moral motivations and might be a threat to morality.

The argument for this is that whatever I do, I aim to satisfy my own desires and my own satisfaction. And when I get the thing I desire, I gain pleasure. Because I do everything to satisfy my desire and gain pleasure, I only pursue my self-interest and that's all I desire.

There's an example of Abraham Lincoln who wanted to show that people were motivated by selfishness in good actions. He stopped when he saw a pig making a loud noise because her piglets were stuck in muddy water and could've drowned.

Lincoln saved the pigs when the person with him asked what selfishness had to do with his action, Lincoln said that he did it because he wouldn't have had peace of mind if he hadn't saved the pigs. So he did it for his own peace of mind.

The problem with this picture is that the explanation why he would've got peace of mind and pleasure from his action is that Lincoln actually cared for the pigs, that is, had a desire for someone else's happiness. Lincoln's argument gets the explanation the wrong way round. It seems like he cares for the pigs because he wants peace of mind and pleasure. The argument for psychological egoism is flawed because it thinks that the object of my action is pleasure whereas that is merely the consequence of my action. There's a confusion between the object of my action and the consequence of my action. In this case, the object of Lincoln's action is not pleasure but the well-being of the pigs and this is what explains the pleasure he derives. He didn't do it *because* he wanted pleasure but because he wanted the well-being of the pigs. And concluding from pleasure accompanying an action to saying the purpose of the action was pleasure is like saying, as William James said, that just because a trans-Atlantic ocean liner uses coal during the voyage, the purpose of the voyage is to use coal.[vii]

Utilitarianism

Now that we've sorted out these confusions, let's look at normative ethics, which looks at theories of morality. A theory of morality explains why any particular action is right or wrong, good or bad. The clearest example is that of utilitarianism, which says that an action is good because it leads to the maximizes well-being in the world where well-being can be understood in terms of pleasure or desire satisfaction. The action will be good because it increases pleasure or desire satisfaction. Let's look at the following (famous!) case:

Trolley: Imagine a runaway trolley that is hurtling downhill towards five railroad workers who aren't aware that the trolley is rushing towards them. You have a lever in front of you which can divert the trolley, but it will kill one person on that track. One dies, five live. Would you pull the lever?

Most people say yes to pulling the lever. But consider a similar case.

Fat Man: A fat man is standing on a bridge over tracks on which a runaway trolley is hurtling down towards five people. You are standing next to the fat man. The fat man is big enough that if he falls in front of the trolley, it'll stop. But the fat man will die, yet five people will be saved. Will you push the fat man?

This time most people say they won't push the fat man, even though both cases involve one dying but five people getting saved.

Since moral theories aspire to distinguish between right and wrong actions, a good moral theory would explain the moral difference (if any) between these two trolley cases. If one agrees in both cases to pull the lever and push the fat man, then it involves performing an action that maximizes well-being. In that case, there is no need for an explanation for the difference between both the cases, since there is no morally relevant difference. The well-being of five is more than that of one. This would be the intuition behind utilitarianism. It seeks to explain why an action is good by saying that an action is good so long as it increases the amount of well-being in the world. Well-being can be the same as desire satisfaction (a preference utilitarian would hold this) or well-being can be pleasure (a hedonistic utilitarian will hold this). The utilitarian would say that in every case where one had to choose between killing a single person and saving five, it is always right to do so.

Observe that a utilitarian theory is a consequentialist theory. That is, the goodness of an action is determined by the best consequences. In this case the consequence is to maximize well-being. A consequentialist theory is in direct contract to a deontological theory, which says that an action is absolutely good or bad, it's right for its own sake and not for the sake of something else like consequences. So, the consequences don't matter. For a deontologist, an action is good because it's done from duty due to respect for the moral law. One's intuition behind not wanting to push the fat man is a deontological intuition, because for the person who says don't push the fat man, pushing the fat man is wrong regardless of the consequences.

What is the justification for utilitarianism? One of the major proponents of utilitarianism in history, the famous philosopher John Stewart Mill (1806 – 1873), argued for it in this way.[viii] The basic argument begins with the point that everyone desires their own happiness as the goal in life and whatever is valued, is valued for the sake of happiness. This happiness, Mill equates with pleasure. In other words, if we keep asking questions like the following chain: why is me playing tennis good or valuable, because being healthy is good, why is being healthy good, because it leads me to be able to do more things, why is being able to do more things good, because they are the things that make me happy, but why is happiness good? For its own sake, because there's no other thing for which happiness is good. Everything else is indirectly valuable and good because it leads to happiness, but happiness in good and valuable in itself. This is an old argument from Aristotle, but Aristotle doesn't equate happiness with pleasure but with flourishing (which will be explained later). Mill rehashes it, and equates happiness with pleasure.

Each individual thus desires happiness as their ultimate goal in life, because for each individual, happiness is intrinsically good. In fact, the individual values happiness precisely because it is intrinsically good. And because happiness is intrinsically good, increasing it is not only desirable for a particular individual who wants happiness, but for more of it is desirable for everyone.

Thus happiness becomes the standard by which not only my actions are to be judged but everyone's. And if my action increases overall happiness, then the action is good.[ix]

In his time, one of the objections Mill faced was about the value of pleasure. If we value mere pleasure, then we are no different from pigs who enjoy wallowing in the mud. We in fact do value things like intellectual pursuits that are more noble and valuable than sensual pleasures, so pleasure is not the final goal.

In response to this, Mill made a distinction between higher and lower pleasures. Lower pleasures are sensual pleasures like eating ice cream but higher pleasures are pleasures due to faculties in us that distinguish us from animals who have mere appetite. He associates higher pleasures with those of the intellect, like with doing philosophy, having 'moral sentiments' and the contemplation of art and beauty.

The reason why Mill says the higher pleasures are more valuable is because people who have experienced both sorts of pleasures would prefer the higher pleasures. People wouldn't trade being knowledgeable and intelligent for being ignorant and foolish. They wouldn't exchange the quality of the higher pleasure for the quantity of the lower one. One may think that they are sacrificing happiness if they go for the higher ones, since it would involve some pain, but Mill says that's confusing happiness with contentment. In this context, he famously says 'It is better to be a human being dissatisfied than a pig satisfied; better to be Socrates dissatisfied than a fool satisfied.'

One major criticism of utilitarianism is that pleasure isn't always good. For instance, the pleasure of a cruel sadist who enjoys torturing people isn't pleasure that is good.

It is also instructive to look at the trolley and the fat man cases now. Judith Jarvis Thomson[x] brings up the case of a surgeon who is so great that every transplant done by him is successful.

Five patients require organs: a lung each for two, a kidney each for two others and one heart for another. If he doesn't do the transplant that day, it's over for them. The surgeon gets a report of a healthy person who's visiting the clinic for a health checkup, and it says that his blood group matches the patients. Should the surgeon take out the organs from the healthy person and save the five patients?

It looks clear that he shouldn't. If he shouldn't kill one to save five in this case, then one shouldn't do it for the trolley and the fat man cases too.

Deontological Ethics

Think of a person, say Neha, who has to take care of a disabled child. The child is so disabled that she'll never recognize that she was cared for. For the person taking care, taking care of the child will only make her more miserable, burdened with this duty. And yet, Neha has a duty to take care of the child (she can't just abandon her) even if it reduces happiness. The duty is such that she has to do it not because it increases anyone's happiness, but she does it because it is right.

This intuition from ordinary morality that someone has a duty to do something because it is the right thing to do is at the core of a theory of morality called deontology. The theory is that an action is right because it is done out of duty, out of respect to the moral law. The consequences don't matter when it comes to the rightness or wrongness of an action. I'll start by focusing on Immanuel Kant's (1724 – 1804) arguments for this in his book *Groundwork of the Metaphysics of Morals* (1785). He was not only one of the greatest philosophers ever, but his arguments for the core of moral thought have been really influential.

The Good Will

Kant claims that the only thing that is 'good without qualification' is good will. What does this mean? A good will is a good intention. The good will being good (means 'valuable' too) without qualification means that it doesn't depend on anything else for goodness and that it's always good. For instance, intelligence is good in a lot of contexts but if it is used to cheat people, then it's not good. So it's conditionally good. The same can be said for other virtues like courage, perseverance and the like. They can all be used for evil ends. They're not always good.

What about happiness? The utilitarian says it's always good and valuable because we can't ask why should we desire happiness. We can't ask that because it is not for anything else's sake that happiness is good. It is good in itself. But Kant says that one may have happiness, but it can still be used for bad ends. One, you might ignore other's people's rights even as you value your own happiness. Second, Kant brings up a person who is happy, but does nothing to control his or her actions by means of a good will. An impartial spectator will see this person as unworthy of happiness. Thus, happiness isn't always good/valuable.

Another important point against any consequentialist theory is that the good will being good doesn't depend on the consequences of my actions either. Suppose some event takes place that prevents me from accomplishing my good will. Or that I tried my best and due to an accident of the gifts of nature, I wasn't sufficiently able to do what I intended to do, the good will still remains good. It isn't dependent on the consequences of my actions.

But when is a will good? Is the good will just like the 'good intentions' when one says 'the road to hell is paved with good intentions'? Actually, it's different. A will is a good will when it acts not based on subjective tastes, likes and preferences but it's without bias and based on universal considerations. If I give marks to students based on my likes, I might play favourites, but unbiased marking is what is good when I act based on a good will. This means that the will is good when it is based on duty, because it respects the moral law.

This leads us to a further question. Why does my action have moral worth or is good when I act out of duty? Kant gives an answer to this by illustrating the difference between an action done *out of duty* and an action done in *conformity with duty*.

Suppose there's a person (Kant calls him a 'friend of humanity') who is sympathetic out of temperament and naturally likes to give to people and gets pleasure from it. Contrast that with another person whose natural sympathies have been reduced due to personal grief, and yet helps people out of a sense of duty. Kant says that it is the latter's action that is morally praiseworthy and has moral worth. Similarly, a prudent shopkeeper gives a fair price due to self-interest so customers don't complain. But it is the shopkeeper who does it from a sense of duty whose actions have moral worth. The prudent shopkeeper and the friend of humanity act in *conformity with duty* whereas the reduced natural sympathies guy and the dutybound shopkeeper act *out of duty.*

What differentiates the action done from duty and the one in conformity with duty is that the former is based on a maxim, which is why it has moral worth. The maxim is the principle and the motive that we have for our actions. The maxim for the shopkeeper will be something like 'Be honest in all your dealings regardless of outcome'.

To summarize. The good will or intention, is good when it is based on duty out of respect for the moral law. But why does my action done out of duty have moral worth? Because it is based on a maxim and not based on its consequence, unlike utilitarianism. So my action has moral worth when I have a good will which involves a maxim as part of its motivation.

The Categorical Imperative

How do we differentiate between the maxims we should accept and the ones we should reject? Kant famously derives the Categorical Imperative as a decision procedure for deriving the maxims on which we base our actions. I'll look at two versions of the Categorical Imperative here. But first, what is a Categorical Imperative?

An imperative is a command. Like 'Stand Straight!' But Kant makes a difference between hypothetical and categorical imperatives. Suppose I say 'I ought to practice hard in tennis'. Now this *ought* is based on my desire to win tennis matches and is better expressed as 'If I want to win tennis matches, I ought to practice hard'. The reason why I ought to train harder is in the light of my goal of winning tennis matches. Hypothetical imperatives like 'I ought to practice tennis' (and this is an imperative because it has 'ought') are followed because we desire a particular goal. But a categorical imperative is one that we ought to follow irrespective of what my goals are and would apply in any situation not just for me, but for anyone.

Now the first version of Kant's Categorical Imperative is 'Act only on that maxim that you can will as a universal law.' Suppose you have a maxim 'Keep your promises but break them when you are hard pressed'. You can't will (meaning 'rationally intend') this maxim as a universal law. Why? Because if you do, and everyone lies when they make promises, then making promises would be pointless. Because no one will believe or trust a promise anymore and the institution of promise-keeping will cease to exist. Since the maxim 'Keep your promises but break them when you are hard pressed' implies that promises exist and the consequence of the maxim is that promises don't exist, you end up holding a contradiction: 'Promises exist' and

'Promises don't exist'.

From this, it looks like we have to obey the maxim because it is rationally required of us to obey it. That means that we'd be irrational if we believe in a contradiction. That's what gives moral rules the sense of necessity. You must tell the truth, and cannot do otherwise. You have to because if you don't, you end up with a contradiction. If moral maxims were based on our desires, then the necessity of obeying them won't arise. Given our goals and desires we might follow the maxim, but we may not, if that goal was different. Thus, maxims are made binding on me, whether I want to obey them or not, and apply universally. And the reason why the good will is unconditionally good is because it's acting from a maxim that doesn't contain a hypothetical imperative.

Note that the Categorical Imperative above sounds like the Golden Rule which says 'Don't do unto others what you don't want them to do to you.' But the Categorical Imperative has nothing to do with what one wants. Also note that a maxim like 'Keep your promises but break them when you are hard pressed' seems bad because of the consequence it has of people not being able to trust each other. But the reason why we shouldn't obey it isn't because of the consequence but because of the contradiction. Unlike utilitarianism, it's not the consequence that matters for Kant, but that keeping that maxim is irrational.

Utilitarianism vs Deontology in Famine Problems

Let's look at an instance of how these two theories work out in practise.

Peter Singer in his famous paper 'Famine, Affluence and Morality'[xi] came up with the following case.

Drowning child: A child is drowning in a shallow pond. At most my clothes will get muddy if I walk in the water to save the child. It is my obligation to save the child and prevent a bad thing from happening, which is the death of the child.

The argument he gives is that if we can prevent something bad from happening, without sacrificing anything that is comparably morally significant, then we have an obligation to prevent that bad thing from happening. In the case of the drowning child, you aren't really sacrificing anything morally significant that can be compared to the death of the child. So it's your obligation to save the child.

From this, Singer goes to a surprising conclusion. He argues that it is also the obligation of rich and moderately rich people to give a substantial portion of their money to charity. Instead of buying that extra shoe or those extra clothes they don't need in order to keep them warm, they have a duty to give to charity. This is because if they wear old clothes and give to charity, they don't sacrifice what is morally significant compared to the suffering of people in the famine.

The reason why this is a surprising conclusion is that traditionally, philosophers have made a distinction between acts of duty and 'supererogatory' acts. Supererogatory acts are those acts over and above the call of duty, which if we don't do, it won't be morally wrong, but these are still good actions. Acts of charity are such acts. What Singer is arguing is that charity is not a supererogatory act, but a duty, and we would be acting immorally if we don't give to charity. His argument also involves a huge reduction in our expenditure on extra stuff and changing the way we live.

Singer's is an argument based on utilitarianism. For instance, one might argue against Singer that by giving charity, one is merely temporarily giving relief, and starvation will happen again and again if the population isn't controlled.[xii] The argument Singer gives against this is that you need to give charitably to whatever is effective for dealing with famine, even if that involves population control. The reason why this is utilitarian is because this argument is consistent with overriding the consent of a population and imposing population control policies to force people to control it.[xiii] Because if that is what maximizes happiness and minimizes suffering in the long term in terms of reducing famine, then that is what must be.

This is where the Kantian picture comes in. Another version of the Categorical Imperative says: 'Always treat humanity, whether in your own person or in that of another, never simply as a means, but always at the same time as an end.' As we saw, something is an end in itself if it has intrinsic value, not value respect to some other end. Things have value because we have intrinsic value that forms the basis for anything having value. The reason why we have this value is because we have the capacity for rational choice and we are autonomous (self-governing free beings), due to which we can have our own ends and act on the basis of the moral law. If rational beings don't exist in the world, there can be no moral worth, since one can't grasp the moral law and act according to it. This intrinsic value isn't dependent on whether we are happy or not, but just by virtue of the fact that we exist. So we are ends-in-themselves, the source of all other value and ought to be treated as such.

What does this version of the Categorical Imperative imply in terms of our actions? It means that we cannot treat people as mere means. When it comes to the trolley problem, given the second version of the Categorical Imperative, it is wrong to push the fat man because we are using him as a mere means. But it's okay to pull the lever because the death of the person is an unintended consequence of trying to save lives.

Just to be clear, we do treat people as means to our ends, like we use the shopkeeper as a means to getting something. But we shouldn't treat people in a way that they are only a means. If I lie to my friend while borrowing money saying I'd pay him back, but know that I won't be able to pay back the money, then I don't give him enough information and make it impossible to for him rationally consent to my action. I treat him only as a means to my end by not respecting his autonomy. If I tell him the truth, then if my friend lends me the money, it's up to the friend to decide so I respect his rational choice and autonomy.

Getting back to famines, for Onora O'Neill, the maxim that would guide us would be something like 'Try to reduce the risk or severity of world hunger'. And we use means in line with this maxim, like even not give food aid if it leads to local farmers having to compete with it and lose their livelihood. Not giving food aid would be consistent with this maxim, but unlike utilitarianism, the point of the Kantian ethic is not whether what we do increases happiness but we treat people as ends.

What does treating people as ends imply? O'Neill says that for Kant, humans are finite in their rationality and aren't perfect rational calculators. What happens is that we are therefore dependent on other autonomous beings and our autonomy is limited as a result. But since we are dependent on others, treating other as ends doesn't simply mean we don't trample over them, but we also act in ways that enhance their ability to act autonomously.

In the case of famines, we act in ways that enhance the capacity of people to act autonomously. On the positive side, this means autonomy can be increased through not only economic aid, but transmission of knowledge for bettering agricultural techniques, improved grain storage, enabling co-operatives, medical systems or contraception, etc. But what also happens during famines is people are more prone to deception, coercion and being taken advantage of. Profiteers benefit from their desperation and sell things at exorbitant prices or loans with high interests are given and people have to take it. This amounts to `offers they can't refuse', that is, transactions in which there is consent but are still coercive because people are desperate.

These 'offers they can't refuse' can also include transnational corporations or international agreements taking advantage of the desperation of poorer countries to get concessions. Respecting people as ends in themselves involves not allowing for coercive action.

For Onora O'Neill, the flipside of utilitarianism is that that it allows for action that overrides the consent of people it'll help, by imposing development projects or as mentioned above, mandated population control policies. This is a problem.

But the Kantian approach to famine in fact highlights its own flipside. One of the problems with Kantian ethics is that it has a tough time dealing with a conflict of principles and duties. Suppose an international organization pushes some reforms, which will actually benefit the country and prevent famines in the future. They do in fact use the 'desperation' to take out concessions for the country. And suppose you are heading that organization facing a moral dilemma. On one hand, you have to act in a way to increase autonomy and not treat people as mere means. On the other hand, not helping the country without the concessions would involve maybe temporarily relieving the famine but increasing the likelihoods of famines in the long run, due to the bad policies of the country which led to the famine in the first place. Which also means that an increase in famines is to allow people to be used as a means even more by other people in the long run.

An older criticism of Kantian ethics is that it'll not allow for lying under any circumstance. On the first formulation, accepting the maxim 'Everybody ought to lie' will lead to people not believing other people and lying becoming pointless. It would thus cease to exist and lead to the contradiction 'Lies exist and don't exist'. On the second formulation, lying is using a person as a mere means. The criticism is that suppose a person is running from a murderer and hides in your house. The murderer asks you if you are hiding the person. Under Kant's view, you have an obligation to tell the truth. But the problem is, you also have a duty to help the person from being killed and not used as a mere means. And this conflict is just like the famine case which you face as the head of the international organization.

Virtue Ethics

When we looked at utilitarianism, we saw that the ultimate answer to 'why do we do this?' was happiness. Utilitarians equate happiness with pleasure which is a subjective mental state. Aristotle asked the same why question but for him happiness, was not a subjective mental state, but an objective criterion for judging a good life, called 'eudaimonia'. Eudaimonia is better understood in Aristotle's own terms as 'living and faring well' or 'leading a life worth living', which involves living in a particular way and is more of an activity. It's sometimes translated as flourishing but that can confuse eudaimonia with just leading a life of pleasure or being rich. However, it's okay to use flourishing if we don't have the confusion.

What is Aristotle's argument for what eudaimonia (or happiness) is? There is something in common in all our actions – the ultimate goal of all our actions which is the final good. The final good, for Aristotle, is the sake for which we pursue all other ends. The final good is pursued for its own sake and we don't choose it for the sake of something else. It turns out that happiness or Eudaimonia is the candidate that fits the final good (or ultimate value), since this is what we all want as the end of all our actions. We can't answer why we want happiness or eudaimonia; we want it for its own sake.

Aristotle rejects money as the ultimate good because we pursue money for the sake of something else, not for its own sake. That is, it has indirect or instrumental value and is not intrinsically valuable. He rejects honour as the ultimate good because honour can be taken away if people don't like you but Aristotle says that 'the good is something proper to the possessor and not easily taken from him'. In fact, we get honour because we have goodness rather than we have goodness because we have honour. He rejects pleasure because he says that it is characteristic of animals but we humans are also endowed with reason and we shouldn't lead lives fit for merely cows. That's why Eudaimonia is none of these and something more objective.

What Aristotle then does is to look at the essence of humans, that is, what makes us human to look at what Eudaimonia is. (Note that Aristotle doesn't discount minimum conditions like a certain level of prosperity, luck, love, friends, external things as conditions for Eudaimonia but he's trying to get to the bottom of it.)

For Aristotle, something's essence is what something's characteristic activity (*ergon*) is, not what it is made of. A knife's function is to cut. And the virtue of something is its excellence (*aretê*) which is its state or condition to perform its function well. A knife's virtue is thus its sharpness. Similarly, the function of a human being is rationality, which makes humans distinct from everything else. And just like a good knife is one that cuts well, a good human being is one who leads a life that exercises reason well. Like the sharpness of a knife, the virtue of a human is for the human to excel in the way he or she exercises rationality.

Since Eudaimonia is the good for humans, just like a good harpist is one who plays the harp well, *the good life or eudaimonia or happiness is the activity of the soul in accordance with virtue.*

What does it mean to exercise rationality well, that is, for the soul to act in accordance with virtue? For our friendships, relationships and the activities we perform in society to go well, we need to be skilled in them. And to apply skill and have good relationships, friendships and to flourish in society, we need to exercise rationality well.

For Aristotle, a virtue of thought is a trait of people's thought, like wisdom, comprehension and prudence and a virtue of character is a trait that's part of one's character. A virtue isn't something you have if you do it once in a while, like you're not an honest person if you tell the truth occasionally. So the character trait has to result in habitual action. Bravery, generosity and honesty are virtues, among others.

And virtues have to be picked up like we pick up crafts. The way a person becomes a pianist by playing the piano regularly, a person becomes just by doing actions that are just. A virtue, for Aristotle, only exists when someone is skilled enough that there is no pain in doing it but it is pleasant. A person who finds standing up against a challenging situation painful isn't brave.

Unlike utilitarianism and deontology, in virtue ethics, you don't act in situations based on a theory of what makes an action right. In fact, in virtue ethics, the question isn't 'what makes an action right?' but 'what aspects of my character will make me a good person?' What this involves is an ideal brave person who is a model and you ask yourself both what is expected of me in this situation, what would a brave person do and how would he or she reason in my situation, rather than asking which principle or rule you ought to follow. There isn't any universal law or formula but what is expected of you in your situation.[xiv]

When Aristotle considers the nature of virtue, he says that it is a mean between an extreme and a deficiency. For instance, courage is a mean between the excess of rashness where one just goes headlong and faces everything without caution and the deficiency of cowardliness, where someone is just afraid of everything. He says that the mean is not an absolute mean, but relative to yourself, so you have to decide to bring a virtue to the situation based on your own nature.

To choose the right amount of virtue involves phronesis ('practical wisdom'). Let's look at the case of the inquiring murderer we brought against Kant. Prudence will require you to bring the right amount of honesty to a situation, which would mean lie and you don't bring honesty at all in this situation to save the person running away from the murderer who has sought refuge in your house. Children, on the other hand, can be too honest in situations and need to learn how to exercise practical wisdom.

One major objection to virtue ethics is that virtue theory cannot resolve moral conflict. A person gets a terrible haircut and asks you how it is. You are conflicted between honesty on one hand, where you should tell the truth, and kindness on the other so you don't. Just saying you should act virtuously isn't going to help you resolve this.[xv] But the philosopher Rosalind Hursthouse[xvi] has a reply to this. A child or young person lacking wisdom won't be able to resolve this. But the person with wisdom won't think that honesty is more important than kindness or the other way round. They'll look at the particular situation and think that it'll not be kind to hide this sort of truth from the other person, even if it is hurtful. Virtue ethics won't have a rule, but it's really important to look at the context.

Abortion and Virtue Ethics

Here's another major criticism of virtue theory. The best sort of rules for guiding action that virtue theory can come up with are ones based on virtue and vice concepts like 'act charitably', 'don't act cruelly', etc., and relies on Eudaimonia and the concept of what is worthwhile. If that is so, then one theorist can start with a different virtue concept from another theorist and come up with radically different conclusions on the same practical problem. Thus, you can't really have a rational basis for accepting some practical conclusion.

Rosalind Hursthouse goes against this by illustrating how virtue ethics can be applied to the ethics of abortion. When it comes to abortion, people tend to argue about two things: one is the status of the foetus, whether it is the sort of thing that can be murdered or killed, and the right of a woman over her body to have an abortion.

On the question of the right of abortion, Hursthouse says there's a difference between the question of legal rights on abortion and the moral permissibility of abortion. One can still have a right, like say freedom of speech, and still 'do something cruel, or callous, or selfish, light-minded, self-righteous, stupid, inconsiderate, disloyal, dishonest – that is, act viciously'.[xvii] The moral right for abortion is thus irrelevant to the virtue ethicist.

For Hursthouse, even the question of the status of the foetus is an obscure question and a virtuous person doesn't have to depend upon 'fancy philosophical sophistication' and what academic philosophers discover. As a result, the status of the foetus is irrelevant to the morality of abortion.

One thing that is relevant to the morality of abortion is familiar biological facts about reproduction that all human societies are acquainted with – that pregnancy is for around nine months, and this results in a baby and that explains how we come into being. The question is now what do familiar biological facts say about the status of the foetus, and how they are involved in the reasoning, thoughts, actions and feelings of people who are virtuous and those who aren't. What constitutes a right or wrong attitude to these facts? This makes facts regarding our emotions with respect to these facts relevant too, that is, facts about the passionate feelings of parents towards their babies and the surrounding family relationships.

Given facts about our feelings towards familiar biological facts, abortion is a serious issue, not like having a haircut where you just exercise a right or do something as a means to whatever you want. The grief expressed over a miscarriage at an early stage is similar to abortion and the even deeper grief at a late stage even more so. To take it lightly and say 'What a fuss about nothing!' is as callous over a miscarriage as over an abortion. This seriousness of attitude doesn't form part of theories like utilitarianism and deontology, because all they're concerned about is just right or wrong.

How does this translate into virtue or vice when it comes to abortion? Given the serious attitude and that something is a vice or virtue in the light of Eudaimonia, Hursthouse looks at some circumstances. Given that parenthood and bearing children generally leads to a flourishing life, a person opting for not being a mother might not be making a virtuous decision. But there can be women who aren't being callous while looking at the intrinsic value of parenthood. Women who have many kids but another one will affect her ability to be a good mother. Someone who has lived a life as a good mom and hopes to be a grandmother. Women for whom an abortion may kill them, or women who go for worthwhile activities in life that motherhood may affect adversely. Someone who isn't ready for motherhood is serious about parenthood too. For these women, having an abortion is consistent with Eudaimonia and so is moral. But having an abortion for merely having a good time or some illusion of freedom or self-realization is immoral.

Interestingly, for women who have bad health or are exhausted from bearing kids or who do work that is physically taxing like crawling in tunnels to carry coal, Hursthouse says that they aren't self-indulgent or callous in their attitude to parenthood. But it's not right to do so and there's something inadequate in the situation since they aren't flourishing. But still, it's justified as there are mitigating circumstances. Because they may still have the serious attitude towards parenthood but they can't realize their ideals as there's something wrong about their conditions in which they live which prevents them.

As we can see, virtue theory gives a complex angle to our decisions way beyond the simplistic divides in our society. But it still faces the problem of cultural relativism, since a culture

Buddhist Ethics

In contrast with utilitarianism and deontology, Buddhist teaching is very practical.[xviii] For instance, Māluṅkyāputta a disciple of the Buddha asks him if the world is eternal or finite, if the body and soul are one and if the Buddha exists after dying. The Buddha replies by giving the story of a man wounded by a poisoned arrow who refused to be treated unless he was told about the surgeon's class, name, height, complexion, address, etc. Buddha says that just in the way that the questions weren't needed to be answered for the practical purpose of healing him, theoretical questions like the disciple's weren't required to be answered to attain Nibbāna, that is Enlightenment.

The solution to the disease that plagues humans comes in the form of the Four Noble Truths.

The First Noble Truth is that all of life is suffering, including getting what one wants and not getting what one wants. It's not an overgeneralization, because even though people might have some respite from it, and joy and good times, the impermanence of life doesn't lead to lasting fulfilment.

The Second Noble Truth is that desire, craving and clinging to things leads to suffering, including craving for existence and sensual pleasures. We get anxious due to being discontented. The three forms of desire are greed, hatred and delusion. This leads to actions like killing, stealing, lies, slander, etc.

The Third Noble Truth is that giving up desire leads to liberation, Nibbāna. Nibbāna, which is the cessation of all suffering in this life as well as in liberation from the cycle of life and death. But this doesn't mean the cessation of all desire, but of those desires that comes from the belief that the self is what is primarily important. If you think that what is yours is most valuable and what isn't yours is less valuable, then you will end up with hatred, intolerance, anger, pride, greed, thirst for power, fame, etc. Buddha denies that we have a distinct self like it's some object you cling to. So if you don't think of yourself as a distinct self from others, your desires won't be what is primarily important. This unlocks compassion for others, and when you are enlightened, you have a desire for the well-being of others.

The Fourth Noble Truth is that following the Eightfold Path is the way to the cessation of suffering. That is right view, right intention, right speech, right action, right livelihood, right effort, right mindfulness and right concentration.

The similarity with virtue ethics is that good actions lead to character but unlike virtue ethics, the sort that leads to liberation.[xix] The other similarity is that the focus of ethics isn't the action itself but the sort of person one becomes.

Like utilitarianism, Buddhism involves a consequentialist ethic, where for utilitarianism, the ultimate good is pleasure or desire satisfaction, the ultimate good for Buddhism is Nibbāna. But unlike utilitarianism, it's not just the consequences that matter but also the roots of the motivation, the motive as well as the action that has been willed by a person. In fact, these mental factors as well as our actions (called kamma) are what cause rebirth and future consequences. It is because of kamma that we need to think of the consequences of our actions on others, society and future generations.

Buddhism, like deontology, involves duties but rather than doing them because of the Categorical Imperative, one does them for Nibbāna and are rooted in reciprocity. While the Kantian ethic is individualistic and based on respect for individuals and equality, Buddhist reciprocal duties and obligations are based on connection to others and compassion and care towards them.

Utilitarianism and deontology have a constraint they need to obey, called impartialism. This means, in the case of utilitarianism, that the utility of every being is equally important, and you can't privilege your own interests.

> Similarly, for Kant, one of the reasons why he wants the theory to be universalistic is that a maxim that cannot be universalized will give one person a particular privilege and that would mean this person doesn't respect others as equals.
>
> A problem with impartialism can be seen in the case of utilitarianism. It makes the theory too demanding for us ordinary mortals. Ordinarily, I have an obligation to feed my kid before a stranger or myself before someone else. Some degree of partiality seems to be okay in our lives because of this. Theories with the impartialism constraint don't seem to allow for this.
>
> Virtue ethics has an advantage that it allows for the virtue of loyalty, which allows for a mother being partial to a kids or doing things for friends which we wouldn't do for strangers. But virtue ethics still has the danger of becoming relativistic. Interestingly, Buddhist ethics reconciles the demands of impartiality and partiality by making the demands of impartiality from monks and allowing for laypeople to be partial.

can still emphasize virtues relative to them that are relevant to circumstances. There have been attempts to resolve this, and you can explore more!

Moral Dilemmas and Psychology

Fiery Cushman and Liane Young[xx] argue that moral dilemmas and the different theories of morality, particularly deontology and utilitarianism are products of human psychology. We have separate psychological mechanisms that lead to these theories. Dilemmas like the trolley problem arise when there is conflict between these mechanisms.

For instance, Joshua Greene[xxi] and his colleagues in an

experiment saw that people had higher brain activity when they responded to the fat man case in areas responsible for emotional responses and social cognition. And when they responded to the trolley case, there was higher activity in areas responsible for deliberative and effortful reasoning. The reason for this that Greene says is that when it comes to harming someone in an 'up close and personal' way like in the fat man case, the thought is more emotional salient than more impersonal cases like the trolley case. Given that personal violence is more evolutionarily primitive than our deliberative processes for abstract reasoning, our emotional responses to personal violence are innate and stronger. The reason why they're stronger is to control us from harming people through interpersonal violence because we need to cooperate with them to survive. That's why, it was observed even in people who said yes to pushing the fat man that they had the negative emotional response at first in their brain which they overrode.

Michael Huemer[xxii] says this is silly because you can create a case with the fat man where it's not up close and personal but you're pushing him with a long pole from a very far distance. But that's not the point. The point is that it is personal violence where the personal characteristics are more salient. For instance, even at a distance, we have more if we have a kid stuck in a well being shown on TV than the suffering and deaths of many kids around the world.

The prediction regarding typical patterns of neural activation was predicted responses in more moral dilemmas which involved saving one versus many lives. Greene and his colleagues gave the following scenario.

Crying Baby: An enemy search party is looking for a family. Should the mother of a crying baby smother it to prevent discovery?

People who answered yes had higher neural activity in areas

responsible for deliberate and effortful reasoning. Thus, Greene and his colleagues made a distinction between two psychological processes involved in moral judgement. First, the cognitive system, which is involved in choices that maximize welfare (which corresponds to utilitarian judgements) and second, the affective system, which prevents you from harming specific people (which is deontological).

In fact, Michael Koenigs, Liane Young and colleagues[xxiii] looked at people with damage to the ventromedial prefrontal cortex. It was seen that compared to healthy people, these people were more likely to say yes to pushing the fat man and smothering the baby. That is, they were more likely to make welfare maximizing decisions, which showed that there are separate areas in the brain for welfare maximizing cases.

Now given that we have these competing systems, Cushman and Young say we can reduce conflict between them and reduce the frequency of moral dilemmas. In order to do this, we can create social institutions in ways that reconciles the demands of the two systems.

But what's more interesting is an application of this when it comes to the issue of affirmative action, or what we in India call reservation. There seem to be social benefits of higher diversity, which makes it good to have this policy on utilitarian grounds. But people also have deontological judgments of it being unfair, especially for those from groups that have higher representation who lose out on admission. This happens when you have a list of applications ranked on race, gender, caste, etc. and then you demote the ones from privileged groups.

But one way of reconciling our psychological systems is to have a different institutional design. Raise scholarship money (perhaps through hiking fees for the rest) so that there can be extra admissions every year and we get these seats allotted to underrepresented groups. So instead of demoting particular individuals from more privileged groups and thus them losing out on admission, which leads to deontological intuitions of unfairness, you do something else. This would be accepted by the deontological system.

What this really looks like is the practical wisdom we spoke about in virtue theory. You keep facts about human nature and circumstances in mind, and make decisions accordingly.

FREE WILL: ARE WE IN CONTROL OF OUR ACTIONS?

What is it to possess free will?

In 2004, Dinesh Thakur, who was working with a major pharmaceutical company, discovered that the company had faked data for some drugs. He had a choice. To blow the whistle or not. Since the choice was up to him, he could have chosen otherwise than he did. But more than that, because his action was up to him, one can say that the ultimate source of his action was he himself and that he wasn't under any compulsion. Due to these factors, he was held responsible for what he did. In fact, because he blew the whistle, he would have been praised by people for his courage. He had the free will to choose... and choose he did.

Our society is built on the assumption that we have free will. Like Dinesh Thakur, we are responsible for our actions because we could have done otherwise than we did. For instance, there is such a thing as an insanity defence for a person who committed a crime while mentally unsound. In that case, the person wasn't in control of their actions, and thus, didn't have the ability to consciously restrain herself. That's why we can't hold that person responsible. Similarly, a person who has been hypnotized to commit a murder couldn't have stopped herself from doing so. So it looks like just in the way we can't hold the mentally unsound person and the person under hypnosis responsible because they did not have the ability to do otherwise, we can hold people responsible because they can do otherwise. This is our typical picture of free will based on which we hold people responsible for their actions.

But what does it mean that someone could have done otherwise? Suppose Rahul has just finished his MBA and has to choose between a big company with a huge salary and good working hours or a small company with less salary and bad working hours and lower future career prospects. But he could have chosen otherwise, and if he had, there was an alternate possibility. The possible situation where he would have decided to go on to join the small company. And the alternative possibility of his life from then on. So there are two possible courses of action that Rahul has to choose from, and thus, two options. This is what it means to say that he could have done otherwise: There was an alternate possibility that he had the ability to choose – more than one course of action. To have free will is to have more than one possible path, and it is up to us which one we take. Let's call this picture of free will the garden of forking paths and the ordinary view that holds this as the **libertarian** view. This involves a single past and multiple possible futures. (Note that libertarianism here isn't to be confused with political libertarianism, which has to do with minimizing the role of the state.)

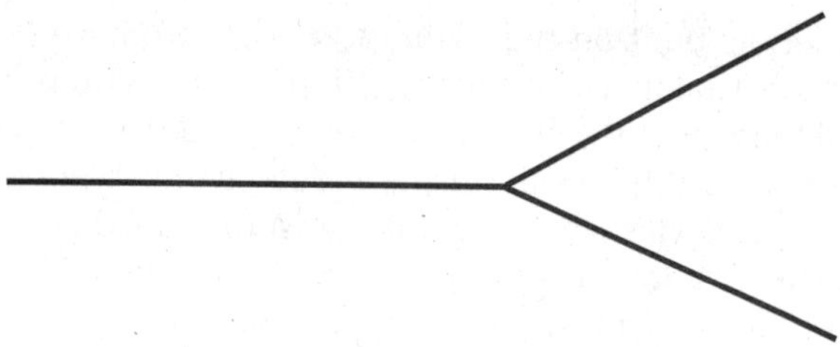

Fig. The Garden of Forking Paths

How Determinism Threatens Free Will

Enter the scientific picture of the universe. Suppose you hit a billiard ball and it hits another billiard ball and the second billiard ball then moves a certain distance at a particular angle. Given the force with which you hit it, the way the first ball was spinning and other factors, there was only one way the second ball could move. The way you hit the first ball and the consequent movement of the first ball *determined* the trajectory of the second ball. Given the laws of nature and the way the first two causes occurred, there was no other way the second ball could have moved.

So every event like the movement of the second ball has a cause, and all the events are governed by the laws of nature. Determinism is the view that every effect has a cause and that there is no other way in which the effect could have occurred, given the laws of nature. So, as a result of the cause and the laws of nature there is only one course of action. In the eighteenth century, a French mathematician and astronomer illustrated determinism by imagining a demon (now called Laplace's demon) who knew everything and could calculate everything. He could calculate all of history, even the fact that you are reading this right now. In fact, if history were to repeat itself, given determinism, events would be no different from how they actually happened. Under determinism, there's no question of what if Napoleon or Gandhi would have chosen otherwise.

So, contrary to the picture of free will that we saw, where more than one course of action is available, determinism entails that there is only one future course of action that is possible. Given the laws of nature and a set of causes, no other event other than the actual effect is possible.

Scientific determinism thus conflicts with our ordinary picture of free will–the picture of the garden of forking paths. This threatens our view of responsibility, too. If our actions are not up to us and our actions are determined by a series of causes and the laws of nature, then surely we can't be held responsible for our actions. Our choices are beyond our control! **Hard determinism** is the view held by philosophers who accept this and say that free will and determinism are not compatible and that we do not possess free will because determinism is true.

To all this, one might say that the current scientific picture of quantum theory doesn't involve determinism, that quantum jumps in atoms happen merely by chance. Things aren't determined, and even Laplace's demon can't calculate the time it takes for a Carbon-14 nucleus to decay. The present state of the universe and the laws of physics can have various outcomes. One might then say that there are random events in my brain, too, and thus we can choose from various outcomes. Here's a problem with this. Suppose your hand hits your nose due to a random event in your brain. But random events aren't under your control, so even your actions aren't under your control. In this picture, you can't have free will either.

The traditional problem of free will is that on one hand it seems to us that we have free will, and on the other, there is determinism, which undermines it. It's difficult to see how, even in the updated picture with quantum mechanics, we can have free will since our actions would then merely happen by chance. In what follows, we shall explore how various responses have been given to this problem.

Classical Compatibilism

Classical compatibilism is a view with a huge pedigree and was held by very big philosophers like Thomas Hobbes (1588–1679), John Locke (1632–1704), David Hume (1711–1776) and John Stuart Mill (1806–1873). It holds that free will and determinism are compatible and that you can have free will even if determinism is true. They think that you can have your cake and eat it too. But how do they even come to this?

One way a classical compatibilist argues for the view is to look at what we mean when we say we are 'free' to do something. When you say you're free to take an Uber to work in the morning, it means you have the power or ability to take it if you want to. And you can't have the power or ability to do what you want to if you're constrained from doing so. You're not free to take the Uber (assuming the cabs are available) if you're in jail or paralysed (hope not!). In effect, from the example, we can see that to be 'free' to do or choose something is to have the power and ability to do what you want and that there are no constraints that prevent you from doing what you want.

The trick (or so it seems) that compatibilists come up with is to give a different analysis of 'being free to do otherwise' than the ordinary view of free will. You are free to do otherwise than take the Uber to work as long as you have the power or the ability to avoid taking it and that there are no constraints that would prevent you from not taking the Uber if you want to. For the compatibilist, therefore, the freedom to do otherwise is just that if you so wanted, you could have done otherwise.

How is this a solution? What you want is determined. Fine. But even if that is so, since 'freedom to do otherwise' has a hypothetical meaning, you could still have done otherwise if you had wanted to, even if in reality you want to do something else entirely. So if the laws of nature had been different or if the state of the universe was different before or both, you would have wanted to do otherwise and you would have been free if there was nothing preventing you from doing what you wanted to. On the classical compatibilist view, you are still free to do otherwise in this sense, and thus, can be held morally responsible. Let's call this picture the garden of adjacent paths. Unlike the garden of forking paths, which has one single past and multiple possible futures, this only has a single past and a single future.

In the figure, the line below is Rahul's actual path – what he actually wants (the part that comes in from above, which includes all his reasoning and what went in the universe before his choice) and chooses (starting from the part that is parallel to the page) The line above is if the universe was different and where he would have wanted (again, the part from above) and chosen otherwise (again, the part that is parallel to the page).

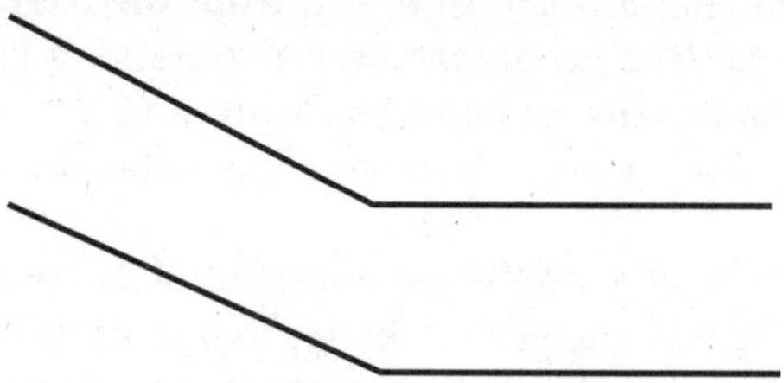

Fig. The Garden of Adjacent Paths

On the face of it, this seems like cheating. How on earth is what I wanted to do in another different world, which has different laws of nature and/or different states, relevant to my freedom of action in this world? Like if I reasoned like Rahul, I'd think, *Either I join the big firm or the small firm.* I'd think in this 'either/ or' manner in this world. It is part of my reasoning in our world, based on which I make my choice. What is the point of me reasoning in the either/or manner if the second part about the small firm is merely a possibility in another hypothetical world? The typical response by the determinist to this sort of worry is to say that even if there's no open future in the forking paths sense, there is a causal difference that the deliberation makes compared to one who doesn't deliberate. The former person's actions would be different. There is indeed a point to our deliberations, even if the bit about same past different alternative open futures might be an illusion.

The classical compatibilist's view is at least in line with some of our intuitions about free will. For instance, if you are brainwashed or hypnotized, there are constraints placed before you to prevent you from doing what you want to do. In that sense, your freedom of will has been taken away from you. And this is their reply to the objection that classical compatibilism does not explain the deeper sense of libertarian free will that we ordinarily hold. At least they explain a major ordinary intuition.

There is, however, another major problem with compatibilism pointed out by the philosopher Harry Frankfurt, who was a philosopher at Princeton University and recently passed away. The view that having free will is to be able to do what we want to do would also apply to animals. But it seems strange to say that non-human animals have free will. It looks like just because one has the power to do what one wants to do without constraints doesn't mean that they have free will, since animals don't have free will. In effect, the classical compatibilist view leads us to not be able to differentiate morally between human and non-human animals since it'll allow us to say that they, too, have free will.

Frankfurt-Style Compatibilism

Harry Frankfurt was a compatibilist. He argued that one can be morally responsible even if that person couldn't have done otherwise. In effect, he denied the Principle of Alternative Possibilities (PAP), that is, a person is morally responsible for their actions only if they could have done otherwise. Now free will also involves the power to do otherwise, and as we saw, was required for moral responsibility. So by extension, denying PAP is also to deny that free will requires the power to do otherwise.

Frankfurt gives the following thought experiment (and these types of cases have come to be called Frankfurt cases). Suppose Black wants Jones to do what Black wants but doesn't want to intervene unnecessarily (and Jones has no idea about this). Black would only prevent Jones in his action if Jones is about to decide to do something that Black doesn't want him to do.

Imagine that Black has done something to change the course of his brain processes (say planted a chip in Jones's brain) in case Jones is about to decide contrary to Black's intention. Now Jones decides to do the action that Black wanted anyway, so Black doesn't have to intervene and switch on the chip to do his bidding.

Now Jones acts on his own and is responsible for his act, but he couldn't have done otherwise since Black would have prevented him from doing so. This is a counterexample to PAP since Jones can be held responsible even if he couldn't have decided otherwise. Thus, moral responsibility doesn't require alternate possibilities. Since free will is required for moral responsibility, you can still have free will, be held morally responsible and yet not need to have the power to do otherwise.

If the power to do otherwise isn't needed for free will, what is? Frankfurt[i] makes a distinction between first-order desires and second-order desires. First-order desires are desires to do a particular action, like just wanting to drink water. Second-order desires are desires to have or not have a first-order desire. For instance, I have a desire to eat a chocolate cake while working. Such a desire is distracting, so I have a desire not to have the desire to eat the cake. In case of a desire to have a desire, suppose I don't have a desire to concentrate on work. But then I have a desire to have the desire to concentrate.

According to Frankfurt, a major difference between humans and non-human animals is that humans possess second-order desires. But for free will, there is an additional ingredient required. You can have a desire without it being effective, that is, it doesn't move you to action. Frankfurt gives the example of a doctor who thinks he can help his addict patients better through psychotherapy if he can experience their desire for a drug. But he doesn't want the desire to be effective, that is, get him to actually take a drug.

On the other hand, there is an effective desire. Let's think of an unwilling addict. The unwilling addict has a first-order desire to take the drug but a second-order desire to have a desire that moves him to actually stop taking the drug. He wants the desire that motivates him to stop to win out and move him to action. This effective desire is what Frankfurt calls will. And the second-order desire that wants a particular desire to be his will, he calls a second-order volition.

So, in the case of the unwilling addict, *his will is not free* because the addict's second-order volition cannot control his will to take the drug. But if the second-order volition is in line with his will, that is if his first-order desire to stop taking the drug wins out, then he has free will. *A person then has free will when their second-order desire is in line with their first-order desires.*

Frankfurt's theory is a compatibilist theory because it is entirely possible for the second-order desire to be causally determined and yet the person has free will because the person can reflectively evaluate the order of his or her desires. What morally differentiates animals from humans is that humans have this capacity and free will, but non-human animals are only capable of freedom of action, that is, freedom to do what they want without constraint. In fact, the classical compatibilist cannot differentiate animals and humans in this respect because, unlike Frankfurt, they didn't make a distinction between free will and freedom of action.

Objections to Frankfurt

One objection that has been raised against this is that suppose a person cheats on his wife based on desires he doesn't want to have. It'll be strange to say that he can't be held responsible, but that is what Frankfurt's view leads to since one's will is free so long as the second-order desire conforms with the first-order one.

The philosopher Susan Wolf[ii] has another objection to Frankfurt. An evil and cruel dictator of a small country, Jo the First, has a favourite son called JoJo. Because the son is close to his father's heart, the son is compelled to be with his father and observe what he does day in and day out. As a result, the father turns into his role model so that when JoJo grows up, he tortures and is as cruel to his people as his father. Observe that JoJo hasn't been forced to do any of this. He wants to do them, and these desires are those he wants to have. But due to his brainwashing as a result of his upbringing, JoJo cannot be held responsible since he has no free will.

Wolf says that in Frankfurt's account, to be responsible is to have one's will controlled by his second-order desires. In other words, one's will is controlled by his deeper self. The problem with Frankfurt's view is that, as per his account, JoJo has free will and can be held responsible since he has second-order desires of wanting to be cruel due to brainwashing, which are in line with his first-order desires to be cruel. His deeper self controls his first-order desires. This is, thus, the wrong result. Frankfurt cannot distinguish between normal cases of free will, where one can be held responsible, and cases of brainwashing like JoJo's, where one can't.

There's also a really interesting argument by David Widerker[iii] against Frankfurt's rejection of the Principle of Alternate Possibilities. Widerker gives a revised version of Frankfurt's case. Black wants Jones to kill Smith. If Jones blushes at a time t_1, he will decide to kill Smith at a subsequent time t_2. If he doesn't blush, he won't. So for Black, Jones's blushing is a sign that Jones will decide to kill Smith. Black doesn't see any blush, so Black knows that Jones will not decide to kill Smith. In that case, Black activates the chip that gets Jones to decide to kill Smith. If Black sees a blush, he doesn't activate the chip.

Now Widerker gives a fascinating twist. Even for Frankfurt, Jones's blushing isn't causally sufficient for him to decide to kill

Smith. I mean, just because he blushes, that's not what's going to make him decide. Something else will have to happen. And the blush does not indicate a state that just because that exists, that's sufficient for him to make the decision to kill. So is it the case that Jones can't do otherwise?

Frankfurt's opponent can just say that if Jones blushes at t_1, then Jones will *probably* decide to kill Smith. But if we add 'probably', then that is consistent with Jones having the power to decide not to kill Smith. Because 'probably' doesn't mean that he must decide. This is, in turn, saying that if Jones blushes at t_1, then Jones will freely decide to kill Smith at t_2. So, not only is ordinary libertarian free will preserved, but Jones also has the power to decide otherwise. The case of Jones is thus not a situation in which he couldn't have decided otherwise and yet be morally responsible. If this was such a situation, then PAP would be false, but it isn't such a situation because Jones can decide otherwise.

Incompatibilism

There are two broad theories about free will that claim that free will is incompatible with determinism. We saw that libertarianism allows for free will. But for free will to exist, they say that determinism is false. That is the only way we can hold on to the garden of forking paths picture. So free will and determinism are incompatible for them. Hard determinism is the other sort of incompatibilism. They hold that if determinism is true, then it cannot be true that free will exists. Again, determinism and free will are incompatible. We will now look at a famous argument for incompatibilism, by the philosopher Peter van Inwagen[iv], called the Consequence Argument.

Basically, the idea is that since the state of the world in the past and the laws of nature aren't under your control, their consequences aren't under your control. Since your present actions are a consequence of the past and the laws of nature (due to determinism), your present actions aren't under your control either.

The argument goes thus (assuming that determinism is true):

Premise 1: We can't do anything now to change the past and the laws of nature.

Premise 2: Our acts in the present are necessary consequences of the past and the laws of nature.

Premise 3: We can't do anything now to change the fact that our acts in the present are necessary consequences of the past and the laws of nature.

Conclusion: Therefore we can't do anything now to change the fact that our acts in the present occur.

The conclusion of the argument simply means that we can't do otherwise than what we actually do since, if we could change the fact that our present actions occur, then another action other than the actual one could have taken place. But we can't do that. Thus, if determinism is true, we can't have free will. Determinism and free will are incompatible.

The compatibilist response to this – to say that we 'can' do something – is just to say that we have the 'power' or 'ability' to do something. As we saw before, to say that we 'can' do something simply means, to the compatibilist, that given no constraints, we would do it if we wanted to.

Given this analysis of 'can', let's look at Premise 1. Suppose I say I can change the past and the laws of nature, which is equivalent to I would change the past and the laws of nature if I wanted to. This is false. I really can't do that, no matter how much I want to. So Premise 1 is true.

But let's look at the conclusion. Suppose my act in the present is that I raise my hand. To say that I could have done otherwise than raise my hand, on the compatibilist hypothetical analysis of 'can', I would have not raised my hand if I wanted to. If the past or the laws of nature had been different, in this analysis of 'can', I could have done otherwise. For the compatibilist then, even if the premises are true, the conclusion of the consequence argument is false, given the analysis of 'can'. Why? Because you can change the fact that your present action of raising your hand would occur since you would have not raised your hand if you wanted to.[v]

Again, the compatibilist runs into trouble. Michael McKenna[vi] gives the thought experiment of a girl named Danielle, who had an accident in childhood that involved a blond Labrador. This trauma made her psychologically unable to even touch a blond Lab. On her sixteenth birthday, her dad brings her a black Lab and a blond Lab and asks her to pick one. She picks the black one.

Now on the compatibilist's analysis of 'can', Danielle would have chosen the blond Lab if she wanted to. So she could have done otherwise. But it looks like, given her trauma, she could not have done otherwise than choose the black Lab. The compatibilist's analysis leads to the wrong prediction in the case, making us say that Danielle could have done otherwise, based on the analysis of 'can', when she could not have. Again, classical compatibilism fails.

Libet's Experiment

In the early 1980s, Benjamin Libet conducted an experiment in which participants were asked to look at a clock and a point at which a dot appeared and flex their wrists. They were asked to note the time at which the dot appeared when they were first aware of their conscious decision to move their wrists. Their scalps were connected to EEG electrodes. This measured two things. First, it measured the Readiness Potential (RP), which was a measure of the gradual build-up of neural activity that led to voluntary movement. The other thing measured was W, the time at which subjects said where the spot was in the clock, which signified their time of conscious decision.

Libet discovered that W was 200 milliseconds before the action and RP was around 300 milliseconds before the time of conscious decision. So brain processes began more than 1/5th of a second/around 300 ms before the conscious decision. Our normal view of free will holds that there is first a conscious decision that initiates the motor response and then the action occurs. This seemed to overturn that. First, the initiation of the motor response took place in the brain, then the conscious decision and then the action. If it's not our conscious decision that initiates the action since it enters too late, then we're just determined by brain processes. The conscious decision is just an illusory afterthought.

However, one can interpret the experiment in ways that allow for free will. One interpretation would be that the experiment only applies to simple choices but not to complex ones in which we reason and then make decisions. And more recently, in 2012, neuroscientists Aaron Schurger, Jacobo Sitt and Stanislas Dehaene[vii] made a telling criticism of the experiment. Assemblies of neurons gather evidence from the senses for an option in a decision and then cross a threshold after which a decision is made. No such external information is present in Libet's experiment before the

> decision is made. There is a random ebb and flow of activity in the brain. If the activity is averaged, the pattern would look like rising trends. It turns out that the time of the decision in Libet's experiment merely happens to coincide with the crest of a rising trend, and this random neural activity crossed a threshold to initiate movement at the time it did since there was no evidence to rely on.
>
> Shurger et al conducted an experiment like Libet's. There was a control condition in which people didn't move. An artificial intelligence classifier was used to see the divergence in the time of brain activity between the two groups. As per Libet's previous conclusions, the time at which the group moved should have brain activity diverging with the control group around 500 milliseconds before. But the difference that was detected was only 150 milliseconds before the movement, which was the time when people said they consciously decided (W) in Libet's. So it turned out that what seemed like a conscious illusion in Libet's experiment was actually the time they made the decision to move. The conscious decision initiated the action after all!

Libertarianism

This brings us to libertarianism, the major incompatibilist view of free will. This is generally what the person on the street tends to hold. This is the garden of forking paths view in which we have free will. For the libertarian, determinism is false, and given a single past, we can have different possible futures. Notice that when they're saying that determinism is false, they're not saying that no events are caused but that not every event is caused.

On the face of it, the problem with libertarianism is this. Suppose given the same past and the same deliberations, motives, desires, thought processes and reasons that led to

Rahul choosing the big company, he chooses the smaller one instead. That is, he might have done otherwise given the same past since his choice is undetermined. But that would show that Rahul's choice of the smaller firm is arbitrary, irrational and just a matter of chance, like tossing a coin. It is irrational because, with the exact reasons that would have led him to believe that the big company was better for his career, it just seems arbitrary that he chooses the smaller one instead.

Along the same lines, the philosopher David Hume also objected that if our actions were uncaused by our character or motives, then they wouldn't be our actions and we wouldn't be responsible for them.

But one of the leading libertarians, Robert Kane,[viii] says the objection on chance merely confuses the meaning of 'indeterminism' with 'chance' and 'luck'. 'Chance' and 'luck' merely mean 'it being out of my control' and 'indeterminism' is actually a technical term that rules out deterministic causation. You can still have causation if a system is indeterministic, just that the causation isn't deterministic. Kane acknowledges that our actions are indeed caused by our characters and motives when they have already been formed and need not involve indeterminism. To even form our wills when it comes to our settled characters and motives, indeterminism has to be involved. These undetermined actions he calls self-forming actions (SFA), involved when there is a struggle between competing visions of what we ought to do or become. In fact, without this indeterminism, we could never have been voluntarily different from who we become.

Kane says that the uncertainty at the time of making the decision is a symptom of the indeterminacy of neural processes at the time. It is this indeterminacy that allows possibilities and prevents us from being fully determined. Suppose a businesswoman is on her way to a meeting crucial for her career. On the way, she sees a person being assaulted in an alley.

She can either wait there and call for help or carry on to the meeting. The uncertainty in her brain indicates that her will is in conflict.

Indeterminism also doesn't rule out control and responsibility. Kane gives the following cases to show this.

Mathematics problem: There's distracting indeterminacy in your brain while solving a mathematics problem. This chaos is like working out the problem with noise in the background. It is indeterminate that you'll solve it due to the chaos in the brain, and yet, you can concentrate and solve it. You are thus in control and responsible despite indeterminacy.

Assassin: An assassin attempting to kill the prime minister has an undetermined events brain that could lead to a jerk or twitch in his arm. If he kills the PM, he is responsible due to his intentional and voluntary action in which he succeeded. The assassin is responsible since his action is his despite indeterminacy.

However, an objection against Kane was given in a disanalogy between the businesswoman and the assassin case. The businesswoman has to make either decision in a responsible manner. But in the assassin case, the assassin succeeds voluntarily due to his will and acting intentionally, but if he fails, it's due to indeterminacy. So the failure was by chance and thus not relevant to free will since it's not a free choice. If that is so, then the agent's (an agent is a thing or person that has the capacity to act) doing otherwise is just a matter of chance, and Kane doesn't succeed in solving the objection from chance.

But Kane points out that in the businesswoman's case, there are two parallel neural networks that are connected, one for processing the deliberation and effort with moral motives and the other for her ambitions. She can then be held responsible for whichever decision she makes because she succeeds in what she was trying to do (the effort represented in the respective neural pathways). And what she did was not involuntary since she endorses that action and decision as her own. Chance or indeterminism is involved as a part of the effort, so one can't say that her making one choice rather than the other was still a matter of chance since the choice was made after the effort. She can still say she did the action voluntarily and intentionally even though indeterminism was involved, and thus, is responsible for it. The only way indeterminism can diminish one's control over actions is like how it does in the assassin case, where he might have a twitch in the arm, and in the businesswoman case, where she is conflicted between choosing two actions. But that's still consistent with their actions being free.

Agent Causation

We saw that if determinism is true, and every event must have a cause, then there is a problem with free will. Our actions are determined by antecedent events, neural firing included, and we have no control over them. If determinism is false, then our actions are random. Libertarians claim that our actions aren't completely caused by prior events and they aren't random. But then, how can we have control over our actions and be free? We saw that the businesswoman has one effort succeeding, but it might just be that her brain events cause her to succeed or they randomly make her succeed in what she was trying to do, and she isn't really in control.

One way a lot of libertarians try to get over this problem is to say that what makes our actions happen is the self or agent that makes our actions happen, and therefore, they're not random happenings. Most compatibilists think that it's just our brain processes and inner states that cause our actions, and thus, we're determined. But agent causation theories hold that there's something, the agent or the self, that is over and above those brain states and can't just be reduced to them. Our actions aren't completely caused by events before them, nor are they uncaused actions happening by chance. There's an agent that causes them that's not determined by events before it.

One major problem this faces is that if the self is a physical thing, then it's part of the causal order, and your actions are determined. If the self isn't physical, then it's mysterious how it interacts with a long chain of physical causes and effects that the causal order is made of. The laws of nature are ones that govern only physical causes and effects. Then does this non-physical self break the laws of nature?

Naturalizing Agent Causation

Interestingly, the neuroscientist Kevin Mitchell and philosopher Harry D. Potter[ix] have come up with a naturalized view of agent causation, based on biology, without the need for a non-physical agent. What they point out is that the actions of an organism are not just caused by parts that compose it (including neurons) or blindly dictated by the environment; the causal power is that of the whole organism, at the level of the system.

The outer skin in complex organisms or cell membranes in simpler ones create a barrier between the organism and the environment outside it. Their internal activity is dynamic, and to maintain their inner processes, get energy, for instance, they're not merely passively affected by things outside, like a rock. They actively monitor their surroundings and adjust to information about it. This prevents the environment from blindly determining everything in it and not merely acting blindly in response to stimuli. This also allows for factors at the level of the organism or agent to cause things. Indeterminacy at the quantum level allows for an open future with possibilities.

Organisms persist due to patterns in the way they are organized and not merely their physical material, which is what leads to them sustaining themselves. In humans, brain processes don't work in isolation, but brain regions signal across systems to collectively enter into a new state. What defines the system is thus the holistic integration and not its parts.

Actions aren't determined merely by the atoms or neurons per se. Neurons and atoms themselves cannot function as reasons for action. What matters for action is the meaning of the brain patterns. The meaning can represent our beliefs (about an object or inner state), desires (goals) and intentions (possible actions). And you can have different arrangements of neurons giving rise to the same pattern. Thus, the higher-order pattern governing behaviour isn't determined by low-level activity, which can be arbitrary. The meaning of the pattern is also based on past learning through experience, as well as our genetic inheritance, which guides but doesn't determine behaviour. For instance, even though genes would guide behaviour, the actions will have to be based on the context, so each individual context needs to be considered. So causation in this case is not just instantaneous but based on reasons that help select one action from possible courses of action. When it comes to humans, we have metacognition, to think and reason about thoughts and reasons.

Potter and Mitchell's picture is thus that the reasons we have at the higher level, which are the meanings of brain patterns and which guide our actions, are not the 'reasons' of our parts, and our actions aren't determined by the low-level neurons or atoms. And since we persist as active agents in our environment, we are not determined by it either. Their picture allows for our ordinary picture of free will. We are agents not determined by our environment but influenced by it, and our actions are indeed caused by the agents themselves. We act for reasons, and we can do otherwise – choose from a repertoire of actions and think about the reasons to do so.

Of course, this might be wrong, but you are free to make up your mind about it.

WHAT IS KNOWLEDGE?

A Definition of Knowledge

Edmund Gettier wrote a paper called 'Is Justified True Belief Knowledge?' in the journal *Analysis*. It was only a three-page paper, but it became one of the most famous papers in twentieth century philosophy. Till his paper, the supposedly standard definition of knowledge was that a subject S knows that p (for example, S knows that it is raining now) if and only if p is true, S believes that p, and S is justified in believing that p.

This is quite a handful. So let's break this down. What does 'if and only if' mean?

An 'If ... then' statement is called a conditional statement. Now consider the following.

(1) If you press the remote control, the bomb will detonate.

The first part of the conditional after 'if' is called the antecedent, and the second part that comes after 'then' is called the consequent. In the sentence above, the antecedent is a sufficient condition for the consequent. That means that pressing the remote control is enough to guarantee that the bomb will explode. If P is the antecedent and Q the consequent, then P is a sufficient condition for Q if 'in the case that P occurs, Q occurs'.

Consider this now.

(2) The bomb will detonate only if you press the remote control.

In this sentence, the only condition under which the bomb will explode will be when the remote control is pressed. Notice the difference between this and (1). In the first sentence, the bomb might explode if the remote control is pressed, but it might explode on its own, too, like if a wire is cut. In (2), however, the bomb will not explode without the remote control being pressed. So it is necessary to press the remote control to detonate the bomb in this case. For (1) it is sufficient to press the remote control but not necessary since there are other ways to detonate the bomb even if you don't press the remote control.

Definitions involve necessary and sufficient conditions. It is a necessary condition for you to be a human that you be a mammal, that is, you cannot be a human without being a mammal. But being a mammal is not sufficient for being a human because you can be a mammal and be a dog. On the other hand, having a ticket is a sufficient condition to get into a concert, but it's not a necessary condition since you can get in with an invitation, too.

In the case of a definition, you have both necessary and sufficient conditions involved. A vixen can be defined as a female fox since something cannot be a vixen without being a female fox (so being a female fox is a necessary condition), and as long as something is a female fox, it is a vixen (so being a female fox is a sufficient condition). So something is a vixen only if it is a female fox (necessary condition), and if something is a female fox, then it is a vixen (being a female fox being a sufficient condition). If we look at the definition as a whole, something is a vixen if (sufficient condition) and only if (necessary condition) it is a female fox.

Getting back to the definition of knowledge then, a person S knows that p if and only if

(i) S believes that p.

(ii) p is true.

(iii) S is justified in believing that p.

The three conditions on the right-hand side of the definition of knowledge were considered jointly necessary and sufficient conditions for knowledge. The first condition is there because it's a bit odd to say you know something but you don't believe it. Notice that this belief is not the same thing as 'belief' when we talk about faith, although we can still believe in God in the sense we're talking about. 'Belief' in this context is on the lines of the belief that the cat is on the mat or the belief that it is raining today.

The second clause about p being true is because if it is true that you know that the earth revolves around the sun, it is also true that the earth revolves around the sun. Again, it's ridiculous to say that you know that the earth revolves around the sun but it's not true that the earth revolves around the sun. This is different from someone claiming before the Copernican revolution that they knew that the sun revolved around the earth. In that case, because it is false that the sun revolved around the earth, it was also false that they knew that.

The third clause is there to prevent beliefs that get to be true as a matter of luck from counting as knowledge. Suppose you randomly buy a lottery ticket and believe that you will win the lottery. It so happens that you win the lottery and exclaim, 'I knew it! I know that I'll win the lottery.' But did you know that you'll win the lottery? No, since your belief just happened to be true as a matter of luck and could easily have been false. That is, your belief wasn't justified. In cases of knowledge, that's why you need a true belief to be justified.

The Gettier Case

Now Gettier comes along and tries to demolish this picture. He gives a counterexample to this[i] (let's call this the Smith and Jones case). Smith has good evidence to believe that Jones owns a Ford. He remembers Jones as always having owned a Ford, and Smith has even been asked by Jones to get into it for a ride. Smith also has a friend named Brown, and Smith has no clue where he is. Now if it's true that Jones owns a Ford, one can also conclude that either Jones owns a Ford or Brown is in Barcelona. Why? Because the 'either... or' statement is true so long as at least one of the sentences is true. This is because if I predict that when I go to Kolkata, either I play tennis or I swim, if I don't do either, then my prediction is false, but it's true so long as I do any one of them. Notice that prediction can be true even if I do both. One, because it's very strange to say it'll be false. Two, because suppose I say when I go to Kolkata, I'll play tennis or swim or eat biriyani, and I play tennis and swim but don't eat biriyani. My prediction is still true, even though two of the sentences are true. (From now on I'll talk about propositions rather than sentences since we believe propositions rather than sentences. A proposition is the meaning that sentences in different languages – like, 'It is raining' in English, *'Es regnet'* in German' or, *'Baarish ho rahi hai'* in Hindi – have in common).

Back to Smith. So, based on his belief that Jones owns a Ford is true, Smith concludes that either Jones owns a Ford or Brown is in Barcelona. He can safely conclude that the 'either... or' proposition is true because one of the propositions in it is true. Now consider that Jones doesn't now actually own a Ford (say he sold it earlier that day), but by quite the coincidence, Brown does happen to be in Barcelona. 'Either Jones owns a Ford or Brown is in Barcelona' is still true, and Smith believes it.

Observe that not only is the 'either... or' proposition true and Smith believes it, but he is also justified in believing it since he concludes it from another proposition he's justified in believing ('Jones owns a Ford'). So his belief that either Jones owns a Ford or Brown is in Barcelona is true, and he's justified in believing it. This meets all three conditions from the definition of knowledge that we saw. But even though the three conditions are met, this isn't sufficient for the belief to be counted as knowledge since it's true merely as a matter of coincidence because Brown was in Barcelona. This is just like the case of one's belief that's true by luck, like in the case of the lottery.

> The Buddhist philosopher Dharmottara (around 770 AD) came up with a Gettier case, too. Suppose it's really hot and you're looking for water. You think you see water, but it is a mirage. When you reach the place, there is actually water under a rock. You had good evidence, and your belief was true, but it wasn't knowledge because you got lucky.[ii]

The No False Lemmas Account

There's another account of knowledge called the 'no false lemmas' account. While proving a theorem, a lemma forms an intermediate step. This account is also called the no false premises account. Let's see what this means.

The philosopher Michael Clark, in a reply to Gettier's paper in 1963,[iii] diagnosed the problem in a case like Smith and Jones to be that of Smith drawing the conclusion 'Either Jones owns a Ford or Brown is in Barcelona' on the basis of a false proposition expressed by 'Jones owns a Ford'. In light of this, Clark proposes one modification of the original definition by adding one more necessary condition for knowledge.

S knows that P if and only if

(i) P is true

(ii) S believes that P

(iii) S is justified in believing that P

(iv) S believes P on true grounds

But Clark points out that there's a problem with this. Suppose Jones actually owns a Ford and it's true that 'Jones owns a Ford'. And Smith listens to Brown telling him that Jones owns a Ford. Brown doesn't lie usually and can be trusted to tell the truth, but in this case, Brown makes it up on a random guess. Smith justifiably believes Brown since he's generally a reliable guy. Smith believes that Jones owns a Ford, the belief is true, he's justified, but Brown's guess forms the ground on which he believes p is true. And yet Smith doesn't have knowledge since it's just a matter of luck that the guess is right.

As a result, Clark modifies (iv) to

(iv)′ S's belief is fully grounded (that is, every ground for believing P is true).

The reason he does is that if Smith were to ask questions about the grounds for his belief, he would say Brown told him. Then he would ask why he should believe in Brown's claim. Because Brown is truthful. Why does he believe Brown is truthful? Because he has always been truthful. Why should he believe he's always been truthful? Because Smith hangs out with Brown all the time and doesn't remember him lying. Smith's belief is fully grounded, Clark says, as long as every ground in this chain of justification is true. In the above case where Brown makes it up that Jones owns a Ford, this makes one of the grounds false (the one about Brown being truthful), which is why Smith doesn't know that Jones owns a Ford.

But consider the following:[iv]

Nogat and Smith: Nogat is Smith's office colleague, who has always been honest with Smith. Smith listens to Nogat and believes him when Nogat tells him he owns a Ford and shows him an ownership certificate as well. On the basis of believing Nogat that he owns a Ford, Smith infers that 'there is someone in my office who owns a Ford'. However, Nogat is lying to Smith. And it so happens that another person in his office owns a Ford.

The above case is a Gettier case since Smith's belief that 'there is someone in my office who owns a Ford' is true, and it's justified, given his evidence. But it's not knowledge since it's just true just by chance. But the no false lemmas account works for this case since Smith bases his belief on one false ground, which is that 'Nogat owns a Ford'. This explains why 'there is someone in my office who owns a Ford' isn't knowledge.

The philosopher Richard Feldman[v] changes the example by adding that suppose Smith doesn't have the proposition expressed by 'Nogat owns a Ford' as part of his reasoning for concluding that 'there is someone in my office who owns a Ford'. What Smith does is consider the evidence, which is that Nogat has been always honest with him, tells him that he owns a Ford and shows the certificate. From this, he concludes that 'there is someone in my office who has been always honest with me, told me that he owns a Ford and has shown me the ownership certificate' (which is true). From this, he directly concludes that 'there is someone in my office who owns a Ford'. This time, 'Nogat owns a Ford' isn't part of his explicit reasoning. Again, someone else in his office owns a Ford, not Nogat.

This is a counterexample to Clark's account of no false grounds since, in this case, all the grounds for concluding that 'there is someone in my office who owns a Ford' are true and justified ('Nogat owns a Ford' isn't an explicit part of his reasoning'), his concluding belief is also true, and yet, Smith doesn't know that 'there is someone in my office who owns a Ford' since it's true merely as a matter of luck.

The Causal Theory

Alvin Goldman was a very influential philosopher. He gave a different account of knowledge to deal with the Gettier problem, known as the Causal Theory of Knowledge. What's more interesting is that he refuted his own analysis of knowledge to come up with a different account, which we'll see later.

In his paper 'A Causal Theory of Knowing',[vi] Goldman limits his analysis of knowledge to empirical propositions, that is, propositions that we come to know the truth of by means of our senses, like 'it is raining', 'the cat sat on the mat'. This is in contrast to propositions like 'all bachelors are unmarried adult males' and '1+1=2', which we don't need to verify using our senses.

Goldman diagnoses the Gettier example by saying that the reason Smith gets things wrong is because his belief is not causally related to the fact of Jones actually owning a Ford and the fact of Jones offering a ride to him. If Smith was causally related to such facts, then that would have led to knowledge. Similarly, Smith's belief isn't causally related to the fact of Brown being in Barcelona, which is why Smith doesn't know.

Because of this diagnosis, Goldman proposes that S knows that P if and only if S believes that P is true and the belief is appropriately causally connected to the fact that P. The reason it has to be an appropriate causal chain is due to the examples he gives regarding perception, memory and reconstruction of a causal process through inference. In the case of perception, I can see a table in front of me because I am causally related to it (and my senses are working properly). If there was a laser photo of the same table between me and the table, blocking my view, I would not see the table because the causal process is missing. Similarly, if I remember that P at a particular time, I do so because there's a belief due to my perceiving P at a previous time that causes me believing p at the later time. So there's a causal process in remembering.

In the above two cases, knowledge based on perception and remembering is due to an appropriate causal chain. Goldman looks at a case of reconstruction based on inference. Suppose S sees lava that has become solidified in parts of the countryside. Based on the belief that there is lava in parts of the countryside and background beliefs about how lava emerges, he concludes that there must have been a mountain that erupted nearby centuries ago. He knows this only because of a causal chain from the eruption of the mountain to the fact of there being lava spread in the countryside. That would be an appropriate causal chain that leads to knowledge. But if someone had removed all the lava from the countryside after the eruption, and a man came in one century after this to make it appear that there had been an eruption and put lava in the right places, then S wouldn't know that a mountain erupted nearby since the causal chain is inappropriate.

Note that in all the appropriate cases of the causal process where belief turns into knowledge, the subject doesn't have to be aware of the causal process to be part of knowledge. This is contrary to what we saw with Michael Clark, where the subject has to represent to herself the justification of her belief.

Goldman, in a paper he wrote later, argued against this analysis. His objection was as follows:[vii]

Fake Barn: Henry is driving on the highway near village fields and identifies different things like cows, tractors, etc., for his son. His eyesight is good, everything is clear, and at the end, he identifies a barn. So far so good. He ordinarily knows that the object is a barn. But suppose there's a case where Henry doesn't know that all the barns around the barn he identifies merely have the façade of a barn that looks exactly like the front of a barn (like in a film set), with nothing behind them. However, the barn Henry encounters is an actual barn, which is surrounded by fake barns, and he rightly identifies it as such.

In the case above, Henry believes that that is a barn in the field, the belief is true, and it's even justified since he is going on the perceptual evidence for the barn. And yet it's not sufficient for knowledge since it's just a matter of luck that he identifies that particular barn as an actual barn. So this is a Gettier case. But observe that this case also goes against the causal theory of knowledge, since the actual barn causes his perception that leads to his belief that it is a barn. But the causal process, which is appropriate, isn't sufficient for knowledge since, as I just said, he identified it by chance and he could easily have been mistaken and have identified the barn next to it as an actual barn.

The Tracking Account

The tracking account of knowledge was famously put forward by Robert Nozick.[viii] The basic idea is that knowledge has to track the truth. This does sound like the causal theory above, like when one tracks an animal, but it's not the same as the causal condition.[ix] His definition of knowledge is:

S knows that p if and only if

(i) p is true

(ii) S believes that p

(iii) If p weren't true, S wouldn't believe that p

(iv) If p were true, S would believe that p

There's a lot to unpack here, so hang on. It's obvious by now why the first two conditions are there. The third condition explains why in the Nogat and Smith case, Smith doesn't know that 'there is someone in my office who owns a Ford'. Remember that the standard definition that knowledge is justified true belief would mistakenly include this as a case of knowledge. But if p were false, that is, if no one in Smith's office owned a

Ford, Smith would still believe that p. So that's not a case of knowledge since it doesn't fulfil condition (iii).

Similarly, in the Smith and Jones case, suppose 'either Jones owns a Ford or Brown is in Barcelona' is not true because Brown isn't in Barcelona (and we've seen that Jones doesn't own a Ford, so the first part of the 'either... or' proposition is already false). But Smith would still believe that the proposition is true because he believes that Jones owns a Ford. This violates condition (iii) again. If the conditional sentence 'if Jones owns a Ford or Brown is in Barcelona' weren't true, then Smith wouldn't believe that 'Jones owns a Ford or Brown is in Barcelona' is false because Smith still believes that 'Jones owns a Ford or Brown is in Barcelona'. So, even in the Smith and Jones case, Nozick's account doesn't count it as an instance of knowledge.

Nozick's tracking account deals with the fake barn case, too. If the barn that Henry identified as a barn was a fake barn, Henry would still believe that it was a barn. Condition (iii) – 'if p weren't true, S wouldn't believe that p' – wouldn't be satisfied and it's not a case of knowledge since even if it were false that that was a barn, Henry would still believe that it was a barn.

The reason why condition (iv) – 'if p were true, S would believe that p' – is added is to account for the following case. Suppose technology has developed enough to put a person in a tank (he wasn't aware that he was being put in one) and electrical signals are fed to his brain by evil scientists to make him believe that he is in a tank. The electrical signals are even fed in such a way that he gets to experience whatever is happening in the tank, and so, the events in the tank are causally linked with the electrical signals. It's a true belief, but even then, he doesn't know that he is in the tank. Because he might as well have not been fed the electrical signal that made him believe he is in the tank and perhaps signals could have been given to make him believe that he is sitting in front of a desk.

But if we just have the condition (iii) – if p weren't true, S wouldn't believe that p' – (along with (i) and (ii)), then it would count as a case of knowledge. Why? Because if he was outside the tank, it wouldn't be true that he is in the tank. In that case, he wouldn't believe that he is in the tank because he wouldn't be fed the electrical signal anyway. So if p (where p is 'he is in the tank') weren't true, S wouldn't believe that p applies, and it would be a case of knowledge. But as we saw, him believing that he's in the tank while being fed an electrical signal isn't a case of knowledge. Condition (iii) gives us the wrong result.

The explanation for the person in the tank not knowing he's in the tank is that his belief isn't sensitive to the truth. In the case of knowledge, for Nozick, beliefs have to be sensitive to the truth in such a way that as facts vary, so will beliefs along with them. Condition (iii) already captures part of this, that if p were false, S wouldn't believe it. But he adds condition (iv) – 'if p were true, S would believe that p' – to deal with the tank case. This gives a reason why the person believing that he is in the tank due to electrical signals is not a case of knowledge. This is because if he had been fed the electrical signals that didn't make him believe he is in the tank, he wouldn't believe that he was in the tank even though he was. So if p is true (that he is in the tank), he doesn't believe that p. Since he doesn't fulfil the fourth condition, it isn't a case of knowledge.

In sum, Nozick's view is that for your belief to count as knowledge, it ought to have been formed in a way that it is sensitive to the truth and track it.

Saul Kripke, one of the most renowned philosophers of the twentieth century, who died recently, had a major objection to Nozick's analysis.[x]

Red and green barns: Suppose Henry is in fake barn county, except that actual barns cannot be green and only be red and that the fake barns with cardboard façades have to be green.

This might be so because the cardboard in the fake barns, due to its chemical composition, cannot be painted red. Henry looks at a red barn and judges that there is a red barn in the field. Now Henry has no clue about the red barns being genuine and the green barns being fake. Does Henry know that it is a real barn?

Henry looks at the red barn and believes that there is a red barn in the field, and his belief is true. So, the first two conditions are satisfied. The third condition is satisfied also, since if it was not true that there was a red barn in the field (in case there was a green fake barn), he would not have believed there was a red barn in the field. Even the fourth condition is satisfied, since if p were true, S would believe that p, that is, if it were a red barn, he would believe it to be a red barn. This leads to a weird conclusion. If you notice, since Henry doesn't know that green barns are fake and red barns are real, it's just a matter of luck that he gets it right that the red barn is a real barn. This is just like the original case from Goldman we saw above. So he doesn't know that there is a genuine barn out there, but based on Nozick's criteria, he knows that there's a genuine red barn in the field. Nozick's theory thus leads to a contradiction – that he knows that there is a genuine barn in the field and doesn't know that there is a genuine barn in the field!

The No Defeaters Account

If you look at the Gettier examples carefully, you realize that the person doesn't know p because there's some fact they aren't aware of. If we look at the Smith and Jones case, Smith doesn't know that Jones doesn't own a Ford. If he finds that out, he would not be justified any longer in inferring that 'Jones doesn't own a Ford or Brown is in Barcelona'. So the fact that Jones doesn't own a Ford is a defeater and defeats his justification because if Smith is aware of this, he is no longer justified in believing that 'Jones doesn't own a Ford or Brown is in Barcelona'.

Similarly, in the Nogat and Smith case, Smith isn't aware of the fact that Nogat doesn't own a Ford, which is a defeater. If he was, then he wouldn't have a reason to conclude that 'there is someone in my office who owns a Ford' and would not be justified in believing this. When it comes to the fake barn case, Henry doesn't know that the barns around the actual barn are fake. If he knew this, this would defeat his justification for believing that there is a real barn in the field.

Given this, one can come up with a simple no defeaters account of knowledge as follows:

S knows that p if and only if

(i) p is true

(ii) S believes that p

(iii) S is justified in believing that p

(iv) There is no defeater for S's justification for p

But Keith Lehrer and Thomas Paxson, Jr. point out a counterexample to this simple no defeaters account.[xi]

Tom Grabit: I know Tom Grabit from the classes he attended with me. In the library, I see him stealing a book and hiding it in his coat. Because of my acquaintance with him, I know it is Tom Grabit who stole the book from the library. Unknown to me, his mother, Mrs Grabit, has said on the same day that it is Tom's identical twin, John Grabit, who is in the library and Tom is right now very far away. It also turns out that Mrs Grabit is a pathological liar, and she's cooked up John Grabit from her imagination, but I don't know this. Tom Grabit was actually the thief.

Why is the Tom Grabit case a counterexample to the simple account? Because Mrs Grabit saying that the identical twin John stole the book is a defeater for my justification in believing that Tom Grabit stole the book. That is, if I was aware of Mrs Grabit saying what she did, I would not be justified in believing that Tom stole the book. So, based on the simple no defeater definition of knowledge, I don't know that Tom Grabit stole the book since there is a defeater for my justification in the belief that Tom stole the book. But given the further fact that Mrs Grabit is a pathological liar, it turns out that I do in fact know that Tom stole the book, and whatever Mrs Grabit said about John Grabit is irrelevant to my justification for believing that Tom Grabit stole the book.

The problem then is that the simple no defeater definition is not necessary for knowledge since I can have knowledge even if there is a defeater. One solution to this problem is to amend the fourth condition to say that there is no undefeated defeater for S's justification for p.[xii] For instance, in the Tom Grabit case, Mrs Grabit's saying that it was the identical twin, John, who stole the book, while being a defeater for my justification, is not undefeated. It is defeated by the fact that Mrs Grabit is a liar who made up John Grabit. So it's not an undefeated defeater that explains why I possess knowledge.

One major counterexample to this analysis is as follows.[xiii] Suppose you buy a lottery ticket and believe that it is not the one that will win the lottery and that belief is true. It looks like you don't know that it will win the lottery even though you know that the probability of it not winning the lottery is, for example, 0.9999. Now knowing this probability of 0.9999 doesn't defeat my justification for believing that it won't win the lottery since it's almost 1. There doesn't seem to be any other defeater either. I satisfy the condition that there is no undefeated defeater for my justification for p. So I believe that p is true, I am justified in believing that p and there's no undefeated defeater for my justification. And yet, I don't know that the ticket will win the lottery for me. We can see that the conditions that the no defeaters account gives are not sufficient for knowledge.

The Reliabilist Account

Reliabilism retains the first two ingredients of knowledge, that your belief be true. But it also adds the condition that the process that gives rise to the true belief be a reliable one. Some versions of reliabilism merely add this as a third condition, and some say that the reliable process justifies the belief (which is accepting the classical justified true belief definition but with a different definition of justification), but we'll more or less ignore this now.

What this means is that unreliable processes are those that give rise to a high proportion of faulty beliefs, and reliable processes are those that produce beliefs that tend to be true. In this view of justification, one doesn't have to be able to consciously access reasons to justify a belief. So this is an externalist view of justification, also like the causal theory and tracking accounts. Its opposite, the internalist view of justification, is the view that one should be able to consciously access the justification for one's belief, like in the no false lemmas account.

The Gettier case shows that the justification that you possess seems internally sufficient, when you possess the reasons for the belief but that isn't enough to produce knowledge. In the reliability view, it's not a matter of you possessing the reasons or being able to explain them whether you're justified. What matters is the reliability of the process.

Now getting back to Gettier cases. It looks like we're getting the Gettier cases due to some flaw in the belief-forming process. The Smith and Jones case is unreliable because Smith's reasoning starts out with a false belief, that Jones owns a Ford, which is not a reliable belief-forming process.

In his paper 'What is Justified Belief?',[xiv] Alvin Goldman provided a theory of justification that was reliabilist. Unlike the other theories of knowledge, which merely helped us count an episode of knowledge as an instance of knowledge, his theory was to explain that knowledge. This is why he added the part about reliable belief-forming processes. His examples of unreliable belief-forming processes were processes like wishful thinking, guesswork, having a hunch and bad reasoning. Vision, on the other hand, is a reliable process, but for Goldman, there are degrees of reliability. For instance, someone believes that he has seen a mountain goat. If the person has a clearer look from close, that person is more justified than a person who briefly caught a glimpse from far away. If we think of the fake barn case, we can explain why Henry doesn't have knowledge. It is because even though he didn't examine the barns more closely when in fake barn county, he should have. That is, his belief was justified but wasn't as justified as his having looked more closely, which is why it was unreliable in the context.

On the face of it, it might look like in the Smith and Jones case, Smith is using a generally reliable method, that is, using a justified belief that Jones has a car and then using deductive reasoning to infer 'either Jones has a car or Brown is in Barcelona'. But Goldman then makes a distinction between conditional and unconditional reliability.

Conditional reliability is applied to processes like reasoning and memory, which are more reliable and produce a higher proportion of true beliefs if their input is a true belief. That is, if the input of my memory is the belief of my having petted a dog named Heidi five days back, and it is true, then when I remember that event, my memory of it (the output) is more likely to be true. Compare this with what happens when the input is a false memory, in which case the output will be likely to be false. So reasoning and memory would be belief-dependent processes. Vision, on the other hand, is belief-independent and unconditionally reliable; its input isn't a belief.

We can now see more clearly why Smith uses a reliable method. Smith has a false input to his reasoning, which explains why he doesn't have knowledge. He is using a conditionally unreliable process. But if he did use a conditionally reliable process, where the input was the true proposition where Jones does have a car, he would be justified in reasoning and would know that 'either Jones has a car or Brown is in Barcelona'.[xv]

One major objection to reliabilism is the Clairvoyance Problem, put forward by Laurence Bonjour.[xvi]

Clairvoyance: Suppose Norman has a highly reliable faculty of clairvoyance. Assume for the sake of argument that there is such a thing that allows one to get knowledge of distant events that we can't perceive with sense organs or any other typical processes. Norman has these hunches on which he forms his beliefs, and he has no evidence for or against the ability of clairvoyance he possesses. One day, on a hunch, he believes that the president of the United States is in New York City. It turns out that he is in New York City. Is Norman justified in believing what he does?

On the reliabilist conception, since the process of clairvoyance in Norman produces a high proportion of true beliefs, Norman is justified in his true belief that the president of the United States is in New York City and thus knows that. But it looks like Norman isn't justified and doesn't know that the president of the US is in New York since Norman is irrational in believing things on a basis for which he has no reason.[xvii] Bonjour says that we can see how irrational he is when suppose there was an urgency when someone wanted to find the US president, Norman wouldn't be justified in acting on his belief.

Can There Be a Solution?

Linda Zagzebski, in her groundbreaking paper 'The Inescapability of Gettier Problems',[xviii] argued that no matter what further condition to true belief, we can't come up with an analysis of knowledge, so Gettier problems are inevitable. Why is this so?

Zabsebski says that any such analysis will involve a strong link between justification and truth. But just because there is justification, it won't inevitably lead to truth. For instance, in the Smith and Jones case, Smith does his best to justify his belief that 'Jones owns a Ford'. But due to an accident of bad luck, that Jones sold his Ford earlier that day, Smith believes in a false proposition. We can see that justification doesn't guarantee truth. Because justification doesn't lead to truth necessarily, we can create a sort of recipe to construct Gettier cases.

i) Take a case of a belief that is justified (or any other condition) enough to count as knowledge but let the belief be false.

ii) Add an element of bad luck due to which the belief is false.

iii) Modify the case by adding another bit of good luck to make sure the belief comes out true. The justification or other condition is independent of the element of good luck.

What you get is a dose of good luck countering a dose of bad luck, where the belief ends up being true without being knowledge. Good luck comes in for Smith when it turns out that Brown is in Barcelona, which leads to 'either Smith owns a car or Brown is in Barcelona' being true. In the fake barns case, you first create a case by making all barns as fake barns so the belief that there is a barn in the field is false. Then modify that so that one barn is real, and as a result of good luck, the belief turns out true.

So no matter what analysis of knowledge you bring to the table, as long as you have justification independent of truth, you can always construct a case in which there's sufficient justification, but due to bad luck, it's false and then good luck is added to make it true. But this case will not be knowledge, so no matter what your analysis is, it'll never be sufficient for knowledge.

Experimental Philosophy

Psychologists Starmans and Friedman[xix] got academics from seven disciplines (biology, chemistry, physics, history, English and philosophy), as well as laypeople to read scenarios that had (a) a justified true belief (JTB) case, (b) a justified true belief case with a Gettier problem and (c) a justified true belief case but with a part that showed that the belief could have easily been false.

All scenarios had the following opening:

> Waitresses at Mory's Pub are not allowed to wear red shirts to work. One day, the doorman Tom sees waitress Krista come in to work wearing a long-sleeve red shirt. Tom goes to the kitchen to tell the manager that Krista is wearing a red shirt. And Krista is, in fact, still wearing a red shirt.[xx]

The above was the justified true belief scenario, too. The following was added to the scenario under condition (c) – a justified true belief case but with a part that showed that the belief could have easily been false, called the Sceptical Pressure Scenario.

> However, because Tom is in the kitchen, he would not have seen if Krista had changed out of her red shirt and into a different colored shirt.xxi

The Gettier scenario had a different line:

> However, while Tom is in the kitchen, Krista quickly changes out of her long-sleeve red shirt and into a red t-shirt.xx[ii]

The sentence participants had to fill in the blank to the sentence: 'At the end of the story, while Tom is still in the kitchen, Tom _______ that Krista is wearing a red shirt.' The options were 'knows' or 'thinks but does not know'.

Philosophers were less likely to attribute knowledge in the Gettier scenario but as likely to attribute knowledge in the justified true belief scenario as in the Sceptical Pressure Scenario. So even if someone might have had a false belief but actually possessed a true belief like in the sceptical pressure scenario, philosophers attributed knowledge.

Laypeople were as likely to attribute knowledge in the Gettier case as in the JTB case but less likely to attribute knowledge in the Sceptical Pressure case. Although, in other experiments, Starmans and Friedman have also observed that laypeople are more likely to attribute knowledge in Gettier cases if the evidence is authentic, like the red shirt case above, but less likely if the evidence is faulty (like the lie that is credible as we saw in the Nogat case).

And academics who were non-philosophers were less likely to attribute knowledge in Gettier scenarios and more likely in the JTB case. Although they were like philosophers in this case, when this was combined with other studies, their judgements in Gettier cases were more like laypeople, where they were as likely to attribute knowledge in Gettier as in JTB cases. However,contrary to philosophers but in line with laypeople, they were less likely to attribute knowledge in the Sceptical Pressure Scenario. Non-philosophy academics were also less likely to attribute knowledge even in standard JTB cases than philosophers and laypeople.

Previous studies had also shown that laypeople were more likely to attribute knowledge than philosophers in Gettier's cases. One of the reasons Starsman and Friedman did their experiments was to examine the claims made by philosophers that laypeople did so because they hadn't spent enough time reflecting on knowledge and the optimal ways to acquire it. But the similarity of non-philosopher academics with laypeople showed that it wasn't a matter of lack of education or lack of reflection that accounted for this. The psychologists wondered that maybe philosophers had differences not because of expertise but because of indoctrination in the discipline.

The Ideal Knower

What I want to take away from this is the idea that perhaps there is an ideal of the perfect knower based on which people make attributions of knowledge. In their experiments, Starsman and Friedman observed that non-academic philosophers were significantly more sceptical even in normal JTB scenarios and were less likely to attribute knowledge even in them. This is because, for scientists, we might be confident in what we seem to know, but we may still be wrong and be surprised. There seems to be an ideal knower then, in the light of which they find our existing attributions of knowledge inadequate.

Think about this. Laypeople and non-philosopher academics are less likely to attribute knowledge than philosophers in Sceptical Pressure Scenarios. Tom is in the kitchen, and his belief could have been false. But if Tom were an ideal knower, it would have been even better for him to tell the manager that Krista was wearing a red shirt in front of her than in the kitchen, given that Krista would not have changed her shirt. Maybe that is why they're less likely to attribute knowledge in the sceptical pressure scenarios. And philosophers who have been indoctrinated by the JTB account lose their ability to think in the light of the ideal knower. They attribute knowledge to Tom in the kitchen based on their awareness of the JTB account of knowledge, where they would attribute knowledge as long as the belief is true and is justified, and justification and truth are independent as Zagzebski wrote.

This brings us back to the options Zagzebski gives, given that we can't ever come up with an account of knowledge that isn't prone to Gettier cases. One option was to give an account of knowledge in which justification isn't independent of truth based on a defeasibility account of knowledge like the following:

'The evidence e must be sufficiently complete that no further addition to e would result in a loss of justification and hence a loss of knowledge.'[xxiii] In this case, you can't have a false belief, because in that case, if you get more evidence e, you'll lose the justification and hence lose knowledge. This means that if you have justification, your belief has to be true. Perhaps this sort of a criterion works for an ideal knower who has so much evidence that he or she can't have a false belief. Almost like God.

In Indian philosophy, the philosopher Jaysankar Lal Shaw[xxiv] looks at what Nyāya philosophers in ancient India would do if they were confronted with the Gettier case. Nyāya was one of the six schools of Indian philosophy. If we look at the Smith and Jones case, Nyāya philosophy would say that justification, truth and belief are present, but it's not a case of justified true belief. Shaw says that this is like the sentence, 'The man with a red iron mask is in this room,' is true not because there is a man, an iron mask and a red object present separately in this room. Smith's belief – 'either Jones owns a Ford or Brown is in Barcelona' – is true because Brown is in Barcelona. His belief is justified because the laws of logic have been used to infer the belief from 'Jones owns a Ford'. But 'either Jones owns a Ford or Brown is in Barcelona' is true due to a different fact, and 'Jones owns a Ford' is justified due to a different fact, which is why there's no connection between the justification and the truth.

This means that 'justified' doesn't qualify truth (like the adjective 'beautiful' qualifies 'mountain' in 'a beautiful mountain'), and the case is not a case of justified true belief. If 'justified' did qualify 'truth', then if the belief is justified, then it has to be true. There is no gap between justification and truth, which is what I said would be true of an ideal knower.

Similarly, in the fake barn case, the Nyāya would say that the physical object is a causal condition for perception with our senses. You don't merely infer a physical object from the way it appears. What happens is that unless one sees the real barn as a real barn (under that particular mode) and the barn façade as a barn façade (in the mode of it being a barn façade), one can't distinguish the two. Because you haven't really seen the differentiating aspects. Since Henry doesn't see specific modes of what they actually are, his belief isn't justified and thus not true. Again, think of it like God, whose belief that it is a barn is true because the belief matches the object the way it is.

The worry that philosophers might have with no gap between justification and truth might be that it would be too strong for ordinary life. A lot of our beliefs are justified even if they don't end up being true. For instance, given the limited evidence people in medieval times had, without telescopes and other advanced instruments, they were justified in believing that the sun moved around the earth. This is why Zagzebski gives another option if Gettier cases are inevitable. That whatever analysis of knowledge we come up with, it'll always have an element of luck, and justification doesn't always lead to truth but usually does. In everyday life, we do make quick inferences based on the way things look, and we end up with truth even though we don't possess all the evidence and even though we might be wrong despite being justified.

I think we can reconcile the two. When it comes to the ideal knower, there is no gap between justification and truth. Which is why non-philosopher academics would be less likely to attribute knowledge even in the JTB cases. Because they have an ideal of an ideal knower in their heads. But the reason why both non-academic philosophers as well as laypeople would be as likely to attribute knowledge even in Gettier cases is that if we aren't clouded by philosophical dogma, we just need enough justification to get by in a world that can change suddenly or have a reality hidden by appearances but isn't usually weird enough to throw up Gettier cases. Which is why there's always an element of luck in knowledge. But even in ordinary justification, we aim at the ideal knower. The closer we get to it, the more likely we are to get to the truth and know something.

SKEPTICISM

This might sound a bit ridiculous. But hang on with me. There's an evil demon who is deceiving you into thinking that the world that we experience exists, even as he's the one generating all your experiences. You think you see a table before you, but it's actually the demon creating this experience. Even the experience of your body has been produced by the demon, so you think you know you have hands but you don't.

This might look like a really distant possibility. But as long as the possibility exists, you don't know that you have hands. There's no way for you to look at your experience and actually distinguish an experience of the actual external world from an experience fed by the demon. Note that it doesn't matter if the probability of this demon doing all this is really low. As long as there's a possibility, however remote, it might still be the case that what you are experiencing is not the external world.

This is just like the following case. Suppose you see something that looks like a rope from a distance but you think it might also be a snake since it looks similar. You can't know it's a rope unless you eliminate the possibility that it's a snake. Similarly, you can't know there's a table before you unless you eliminate the possibility that you're not being deceived by a demon. So the argument is:

Premise 1: If you have knowledge of the external world, then you know that you are not being deceived by a demon.

Premise 2: You don't know you aren't being deceived by a demon.

Conclusion: Therefore, you don't have knowledge of the external world.

You might feel as if the ground beneath your feet is slipping. This is a form of sceptical doubt, and remember, a doubt occurs when you entertain the possibility that your belief might be false. This is one such form of radical doubt on the basis of which Rene Descartes (1596–1650) in his *Meditations on First Philosophy*[i] doubted not only our beliefs about the external world but also basic knowledge of truths of mathematics like 2 and 2 equals 4. His quest was to find a certain foundation for all knowledge by doubting everything. The foundation, then, would be the truths that are immune to doubt.

There's a contemporary version of this.[ii] Suppose scientists have developed a technology that can wire people's brains to a computer and feed them electrical impulses that give the same experiences that they would have if they were experiencing actual objects around them. Imagine that your brain is in a vat and is connected in this manner. Your experiences are indistinguishable from what you would experience if you were sensing things in the external world. That's why you don't know that you are not a brain-in-a-vat (BIV). So when it comes to brains in vats, the argument for scepticism about knowledge of the external world becomes:

Premise 1: If you have knowledge of the external world, then you know that you are not a brain-in-a-vat.

Premise 2: You don't know you aren't a brain-in-a-vat.

Conclusion: You don't have knowledge of the external world.

How do we get out of this mess? We'll look at a few solutions. But what's more important is that these solutions give us insights into the nature of language and how we get to know stuff, which is why this whole thing isn't as ridiculous as it sounds.

The Inference to the Best Explanation Solution

One day, Mahesh comes home to discover that the lock to his door has been broken and all the valuables in his locker have disappeared. There can be different possible explanations or hypotheses. One is that his wife has taken them. But that does not explain why the lock is broken. If she has the key, then why would she break the lock? That's why the hypothesis that his wife did it does not explain all relevant observations. If the wife stole it and left him, the explanation needs another explanation. So the explanation is shallow since the explanation can only go this far. Why would she leave him this way without informing him and breaking the lock if everything was fine between them? The answers are obscure. Suppose the proposed explanation is that the Income Tax Department has a device that can detect illegal wealth and teletransport it, and sometimes it malfunctions and takes legal wealth, too. The problem is that this explanation is too complicated. The property of a good explanation is that it makes as few assumptions as possible. If you can explain this event with a simpler explanation, then the simpler one ought to be favoured. In this case, the best explanation for Mahesh is that robbers stole his money.

We make inferences to select the best explanation for a particular phenomenon. The process of reasoning involved in choosing this best explanation is called inference to the best explanation or abduction. The form an abductive argument takes is as follows:

Phenomena p.

Hypothesis h explains p.

No other hypothesis explains p as well as h.

Therefore, it's probable that h is true.

The sceptical problem arises because of the underdetermination principle, which is a general principle of knowledge. If there are two competing hypotheses and all the information you have doesn't allow you to choose one hypothesis as the better one, then you don't know that either of them is the case. Suppose someone says that there is water on Mars. Water might have come about a long time back and it's still there, or due to the difference in its surface and temperatures, it disappeared. But there's no way to decide between the claim that there's water on Mars or no water since there's no information about it from space probes sent there. Given the absence of information to choose one claim or the other, we don't know that there's water on Mars, and we don't know that there isn't either.[iii]

Similarly, the brain-in-a-vat hypothesis gives us two hypotheses. One is that the world is the source of our experiences, and the other is that a computer is the source and that you have been deceived. Given the information from your experiences and there being nothing to distinguish in them to settle the matter, you don't know whether either of them is true. That's the basis for Premise 2, that is, you don't know you aren't a brain-in-a-vat.

Let's call the explanation of our sensory experiences based on our ordinary beliefs, which says that the world is the source of our experiences, the Real-World Hypothesis. The Sceptical Hypothesis is the explanation of our sensory experiences based on the sceptical scenarios: that the demon or the computer generates our experiences.

Jonathan Vogel, like many others before him, including the philosopher Bertrand Russell, argue, that the real-world hypothesis best explains our experiences rather than the

Sceptical Hypothesis. The strategy to deal with scepticism thus involves inference to the best explanation. How does that work?

You're looking at a computer. The real-world hypothesis explains your experience by saying that you have this experience because the computer is in front of you, you have adequate light to see it, your eyes aren't shut and that's why you can see it. On the other hand, Vogel considers one version of a sceptical hypothesis, which is the Minimal Sceptical Hypothesis. This hypothesis is that your experience of looking at a computer in front of you is caused *unveridically*, which means that its cause is other than what you think. But this hypothesis doesn't have anything to say about how or why you have the experience. Since it doesn't offer any explanation of your experience, it's flawed because it is an ad hoc explanation.

What does an ad hoc explanation mean? Vogel gives the example of Dr G who diagnoses Roger's symptoms of sneezing, moist eyes and it happening at a particular time of the year as an allergy. The hypothesis that it is an allergy is better than it being a chronic respiratory infection or a cold because it explains the symptoms better. But suppose someone just comes in and says that something apart from the allergy is causing the symptoms but doesn't say why. This hypothesis doesn't explain anything about why or how the symptoms are caused because it's just a shallow and bare hypothesis and an ad hoc explanation. In fact, the minimal sceptical hypothesis is just like this, in that there is no explanation as to why or how. There's no reason for us to reject our ordinary beliefs, just like Dr G. doesn't need to reject the explanation that it is an allergy.

But suppose there is a more complicated hypothesis that tries to match the successful nature of the Real-World Hypothesis. Vogel calls this the Isomorphic Sceptical Hypothesis. Suppose you see a cat eating. The computer feeding you this experience has a file for cat and with *the cat is eating* being an entry in it. When in your experience, a cat stops eating and starts grooming, the file is updated with the entry replaced by *the cat is grooming*, which causes your experience. So what you get is that the computer gives you a simulation feature by feature. The explanation is now not ad hoc; it gives you the why and how of your experiences.

Of course, there's a problem with this, too. In the Real-World Hypothesis, we attribute properties to objects, like the property of *being round* to a peg when we see a round peg. The real-world hypothesis explains the peg's behaviour as a round object, like it looks round, fits into round holes, etc., because it actually is round. But the isomorphic sceptical hypothesis has a way more complicated explanation and has to explain why something that is not round behaves like it does. Not only does the computer file not behave like something round because it isn't round, but you also need to give a roundabout complicated explanation of why it systematically behaves as if it were something round. And remember, a feature of a more acceptable hypothesis is that it should be less and not needlessly complicated. Thus, the Real-World Hypothesis is a better one.

To illustrate, Vogel gives a contrast between the round earth hypothesis and the flat earth hypothesis, held by a weird bunch of people called flat earthers. The Earth behaves like something round since if a traveller went all the way in a single direction, she'll get back to where she started. The round earth hypothesis explanation is that this is because the Earth is actually round. Flat earthers have to give complicated explanations like saying that the moon landing and images supposedly from there are fake. And it gets even messier when it has to explain why navigational devices and compasses systematically mislead people. For Vogel, the minimal Sceptical hypothesis was rejected because it didn't say enough, the isomorphic sceptical hypothesis should be rejected because, like the flat earth hypothesis, it says too much.

Susanna Rinard has a simple objection to the sort of argument

Vogel is making.[iv] We saw that Vogel's argument against the Isomorphic Sceptical Hypothesis is that it involves a more complicated explanation of why the peg is round. There's also an argument that people who hold the inference to the best explanation view have: the reason objects behave regularly and have continuity in our experiences is because there is a world out there that is regular and there are, in fact, objects that are continuous and any other explanation is more complicated. The reason why the peg exists continuously without disappearing randomly and behaves in particular ways with other objects like not flying off suddenly is because there are laws of nature that explain its regularity.

But is the Real-World Hypothesis actually the best explanation? In fact, one can have a simpler explanation than saying there is an extra realm of objects (the external world) apart from our experiences. There's a view called Idealism, which says that the world and all the objects that exist in it aren't material, but they are all ideas that exist in people's minds. Now the reason why it's a simpler explanation to say that the round peg just exists as an idea in our experience and there's no external world that is material is because there is one less extra realm of objects. And the Idealist Hypothesis can just say that the regularity exists because there are laws that just apply to the realm of experience.

One objection that Susanna Rinard imagines is that the Real-World Hypothesis can just say that our experiences are not sufficient to explain why something is continuous. For instance, suppose in the centre of your visual field there's a brown square shape that's stationary. From the left of the visual field, a round black shape appears and vanishes gradually where the stationary brown shape is. It then reappears part by part on the other side of the brown square shape and moves ahead to the right side of the visual field. Your experience itself is discontinuous when the black round shape disappears, but the discontinuity in experience is explained by saying that the black round shape was actually continuous but was behind the brown shape. So you need external material objects to explain why your experience is discontinuous, and that's a simpler explanation.

But Rinard replies that even if this is right, the Idealist Hypothesis is still simpler because whereas the real-world hypothesis holds that innumerable objects in the world exist apart from the mind, idealism holds that only minds do. The Idealist Hypothesis also holds that the only kind of objects are the ones that exist in experience, so there are fewer kinds of objects. Also, the laws are fewer in idealism because the Real-World Hypothesis not only has laws governing interaction between physical objects but also between physical objects and experience. That's how there's an explanation of how you have an experience of a round object. But for Idealism, you only need laws that apply to experience and no laws that relate experiences to an additional realm. That's why the Idealist Hypothesis is simpler and a better explanation than the Real-World Hypothesis.

The Moorean Response

There's another sort of response, which was made by G.E. Moore,[v] one of the stalwarts of twentieth-century philosophy. Suppose A says that there are three misprints on a particular page of a book and B doubts this. To prove that he is right, A takes the book, goes to the page and says, 'There's a misprint here, and here and another here.' Thus, there are three misprints. Similarly, Moore says that to prove that two humans exist, he gestures with his left hand and says, 'Here is one hand' and gestures with the right, saying, 'Here is another.' But by doing so, he not only proves that two human hands exist, but that since they exist, external objects exist, too.

This sounds so neat. In fact, Moore's proof of the external world satisfies the requirements for what a proof ought to have. The first requirement is that the conclusion ought to be different from the premise, that is, it should not beg the question. Begging the question means to assume in your premises the point that is being contended. For instance, suppose a person who has been accused of murder is referred to by the prosecutor as 'the murderer'. The prosecutor thus assumes the point at issue is that the accused is the murderer, whereas the issue is to actually establish that the person is the murderer. So the lawyer begs the question that the accused is the murderer even though that is yet to be shown.[vi] In Moore's argument, he doesn't assume what he's trying to prove, that is, he's not assuming that there are two hands. As a result, the conclusion is different from what is in the premises of his argument. If he had begged the question, its premise would have said what's in the conclusion, just like the lawyer assumes in his premise that the person is the murderer, but that is what is to be shown only in the conclusion.

The other condition to be satisfied by an adequate proof is that he knows the premise to be true, not just something that he believes and is not certain about. It also seems absurd to deny that he didn't know that he had a hand because his eyes were wide open and he was looking at his hand in the light just like the person looking at the misprint didn't have anything wrong with his senses. The third condition is that the conclusion needs to follow from the premise. This means that the argument has to be a valid one. To remind you, an argument is valid when and if the premises are true; then the conclusion cannot fail to be true. For instance, let's look at the following argument.

Premise 1: All dolphins are mammals.

Premise 2: Toby is a dolphin.

Conclusion: Toby is a mammal.

To say that the conclusion follows from the premises is also to say that the premises entail the conclusion.

Now contrast this with an invalid argument.

Premise 1: All dolphins are mammals.

Premise 2: Toby is a mammal.

Conclusion: Toby is a dolphin.

In the second argument, if the premises are true, there is a possibility of the conclusion being false. For instance, if Toby was a dog, which is a mammal, Toby would not be a dolphin. But in the first argument, it's not conceivable in a world where the premises are true that the conclusion is false. It's just not possible.

Note that the premises don't have to be true for an argument to be valid. Consider the following:

Premise 1: All dolphins can fly.

Premise 2: Toby is a dolphin.

Conclusion: Therefore, Toby can fly.

The premises are false, but if they were true, it would not be possible for the conclusion to be false. If the argument was valid, and if all the premises are in fact true, then it is a sound argument. What Moore claims is that this argument is not only valid but that it is also sound, that is, all his premises are true. His argument for the external world satisfies all the conditions for a proof.

One objection to Moore that he anticipates is that he doesn't know the premises that he has a hand and another hand because he hasn't yet proved this. But Moore replies that he can still know things he can't prove. For instance, investigators have seen a murderer, so they know it, but they can't prove it in court because all the key records have been burnt down.[vii] Children can know lots of things about the world, but they might not be able to give reasons why. Yet, they still know them.

A major objection to Moore's argument is from Crispin Wright,[viii] who argues that it still begs the question. Consider the following inference.

Toadstool:

I Three hours ago, Jones inadvertently consumed a large risotto of *Boletus satanas*.

II Jones has absorbed a lethal quantity of the toxins that a toadstool mushrooms contains.

Therefore:

III Jones will die shortly.

In this, the first proposition is good evidence for the second one, even though it's defeasible. It being defeasible means that if the first proposition is true, then the second proposition can still be false. The quantity might not be lethal if, for instance, Jones has taken an antidote. But the second proposition entails the third: If the second is true, it cannot be false that Jones will die because the quantity was by definition lethal. But what is important about this is that the support that the first proposition gives for the second one also transmits through the entailment from the second to the third. What this means is that because Jones consuming the large risotto of toadstool mushrooms (first) is evidence for it being a lethal quantity of toxins (second), it is also evidence for Jones shortly dying (third).

Now consider this.

Election:

I Jones has just placed an X on a ballot paper.

II Jones has just voted.

Therefore:

III An election is taking place.

The election case seems just like the toadstool case, where the first proposition is good evidence for the second and yet defeasible. It also looks like the evidence the first provides for the second is also provided for the proposition entailed by the second. Jones placing an X on a ballot paper is evidence of him having voted and there being an election.

But Wright says that this isn't right. Suppose a society holds election drills that are like fire drills, held as regularly as proper elections are held. It is equally likely that Jones is taking part in a drill than an actual election. What then happens is that Jones placing an X on a ballot paper is not evidence any more for his voting. If a drill is as likely as an election, then Jones placing an X on a ballot paper is not a better reason to think he actually voted than that he didn't.

It is only if you have independent reason to believe in III, that an election is taking place, that Jones placing an X on a ballot paper (I) is evidence of him having just voted (II). If you have evidence to believe that an election is happening, you'll also have evidence to believe that the mark X on the paper is a vote. So, on its own, the ground that the first proposition provides for the second doesn't transmit from the second to the third. Since on its own, Jones marking X on a ballot paper is not a good reason to believe that he is voting, it's not a good reason to believe there is an election occurring.

Wright now reformulates Moore's argument as:

MORE*

I My experience is in all respects as of a hand held up in front of my face.

II Here is a hand.

Therefore:

II There is a material world.

(Since any hand is a material object existing in space)

In order to show that there is a material world, Moore has to show that the defeasible evidence from his experience (first proposition) for the second proposition (that there is a hand) is also evidence for there being a material world. In other words, he needs to show that the support MORE* I provides for MORE* II transmits to MORE* III. But the sceptic can point out that Moore's experience can only provide the sort of evidence that he has a hand only if Moore already holds that the material world is the most likely cause of his experience. Unless he already has evidence for the material world, his experience that seems like a hand cannot provide evidence that there is actually a hand. This is just like the election case, where unless one already has evidence that there is an election going on, Jones making a mark on the ballot paper cannot provide evidence that he has voted. As a result, Moore is begging the question and thus assumes what he has to prove because his argument assumes the existence of the material world to prove there is a material world.

Semantic Externalism

One of the things semantics studies is the nature of the meaning of words. Hilary Putnam[ix] had a famous thought experiment based on which he argued that the meaning of our words and what our thoughts are about (their content) are not just a matter of what is going on in our heads. This means that there has to be a causal connection between our use of a word and things in the world. To illustrate, let's look at a famous thought experiment that Putnam uses.

Twin Earth: There is another planet somewhere in the galaxy. Let's call it 'Twin Earth' since everything is similar to Earth and people even speak English. You even have a body double there. The main difference is that that which is referred to by the word 'water' is not H_2O but a compound for which the formula is XYZ. The coincidence is that it behaves like our water, is transparent, boils at the same temperature, etc. If a spaceship from our Earth visits Twin Earth and discovers what the substance is, they'll say that 'water' on Twin Earth means XYZ. Now suppose there's an Oscar on Earth in 1750, before people knew that water was H_2O, and a Twin Oscar on Twin Earth who looks like Oscar and whose psychological states appear to be the same as Oscar. Does he mean the same thing when he says 'water' on Twin Earth as Oscar on Earth?

The intuition is that no, even then they refer to two different liquids since the lakes on Twin Earth are composed of XYZ and those on Earth of H_2O. Thus, the meanings of our words are determined at least partly by the nature of what they are causally connected to. This thesis is called semantic externalism.

Here's Putnam's argument against scepticism. If you are a brain in a vat, and you think, *I'm a brain in a vat,* then the word 'brain' refers to the image of the brain that the computer has generated for you or electrical impulses or features in the program that cause it. In vat-English, the words 'brain' and 'vat' refer to different things than in English since they're not causally connected to actual vats or brains.

In light of this, if you in the vat think, *I'm a brain in a vat* (which means I'm a brain in a vat in the image), then that is false. It is false because you're not the image of the brain in a vat that the words mean but an actual brain in a vat. So, if you are a brain in a vat, your saying, 'I'm a brain in a vat' cannot possibly be true. And if you're not a brain in a vat and you think, *I'm a brain in a vat,* that is false, too, since you're not actually a brain in a vat. Either way, it is always false when you say, 'I'm a brain in vat.' Whenever you utter, 'I'm a brain in a vat,' it is always false. That way, you can't ever be a brain in a vat! Not only that, the argument is self-defeating since, if you were a brain in a vat, you couldn't even entertain that possibility because it'll mean 'I'm a brain in a vat in the image'.

A major objection to this picture[x] is to say that Putnam's argument eliminates only some sorts of sceptical scenarios, like if your brain has always been in a vat. But it doesn't get rid of the possibility of another. Suppose you have grown up using the word 'brain' for actual brains and 'vat' for actual vats. But you then get kidnapped by an evil scientist who puts your brain in a vat with you not knowing that you have been kidnapped. After that, the simulations that are fed to you are what seems like a continuity.

In the above case, you are using 'brain-in-a-vat' to refer to an actual brain in a vat and actually considering the possibility that you are that, unlike in Putnam's argument. In that case, saying, 'I'm a brain in a vat' is not false because you're not referring to the image of a brain in a vat. This sort of sceptical possibility is still left open by Putnam's argument.

Contextualism

Another attempted solution to the problem of scepticism is a view known as contextualism. This view holds that the standards for what counts as an instance of knowledge change with context, that is, with different settings and situations. What this means is that in a certain context, the standard for what makes 'S knows that p' (remember from the last chapter that S is a subject and p is a proposition) true might be high; in other contexts, it may be lower, and the standards can vary along a spectrum. Let's see what this means and how it tries to deal with scepticism. Keith DeRose[xi] gives the following cases:

Bank Case A: DeRose and his wife are driving in front of the bank on Friday afternoon. They were supposed to drop their salary cheques but discover that the line is really long in the bank. Even though they prefer to deposit their cheques immediately after receiving their salary, DeRose tells his wife that it's not really urgent that it be deposited immediately, so they can put the cheques in on Saturday. His wife says that since many banks are shut on Saturdays, it might be that this one won't be open, too. To which DeRose replies that he knows that it will be open since he was there two Saturdays back.

Bank Case B: DeRose and his wife are in the same situation as above, except that this time, it's really urgent to deposit the cheques because if they don't deposit them, a cheque for a big amount they have written will bounce on Monday. Since banks are closed on Sundays, they'll be in trouble. DeRose suggests that they can deposit it on Saturday since he was at the bank two weeks back on Saturday and it was open. But the wife reminds him why it's urgent and says that banks do change the hours they work. Upon being asked whether he knows the bank will be open on Saturday, even though he is confident, he replies that he doesn't know and it's better they go in to double-check.

It looks like in both cases, DeRose is telling the truth. In Bank Case A, it is true that he knows that the bank will be open on Saturday, and in Bank Case B, it is true that he does not know that the bank will be open on Saturday. His knowing and not knowing seem to contradict each other. But in the first case, the possibility of the bank being closed is not considered, and his justification doesn't need to be that strong for it to be true that he knows. What happens is that the context determines a low standard for what counts as knowledge, that is, in this case, the degree of justification he possesses doesn't need to be really high for his belief to be knowledge. That's why, relative to the low standard in this context, he knows that the bank will be open on Saturday. But in Bank Case B, the wife's mention of the possibility that the bank might be closed on Saturday and the urgency that shows the high stakes involved raises the epistemic (fancy word that means 'of or relating to knowledge') standard. Thus, relative to the standards in this context, it is true that he doesn't know that the bank is open on Saturday.

Contextualism says that, look, there is no standard for what counts as an instance of knowledge that's absolute and independent of context. That's why DeRose's knowing in Case A that the bank will be open on Saturday and not knowing in Case B don't really contradict each other.

Think of a word like 'tall'. Suppose I go to a village in Uttar Pradesh and want a good view of the surroundings. I look at a four-storey building and say it is tall. But if a person from Mumbai comes along and says that there are no tall buildings here, he's not really contradicting me. Relative to the standards to determine the tallest building in the area, the building is tall, but when the standards for what counts as tall are raised, relative to the skyscrapers in Mumbai, it is not tall.[xii] And it's not that there are two completely different senses of the verb 'knows' in different contexts like 'bank' (in one sense it is a financial institution and in another can be the bank of a river). It's more like there is a common core meaning for words like 'I' (the person speaking) and 'here' (the current place), but its sense varies the way – 'here' can be Mumbai when you're in Mumbai or Kolkata when you're there.

Similarly, contextualists say that it is true in ordinary contexts when you say that you know you have a hand. But the sceptic raises the standard when the BIV possibility becomes salient, which is why you don't know that you have a hand relative to the standards in the sceptical context. How does this deal with the sceptical problem? Consider the argument by the sceptic again.

Premise 1: If you have knowledge of the external world, then you know that you are not a brain-in-a-vat (BIV).

Premise 2: You don't know you aren't a brain-in-a-vat.

Conclusion: You don't have knowledge of the external world.

The contextualist would say that in the sceptic's high standard context, the argument is a sound one, that is, it is both valid and all the premises are true. In that context, the conclusion is true, but it would be an overgeneralization to say that the conclusion is true in ordinary contexts, too.[xiii] Relative to lower standards in ordinary contexts, say when you are asked if you know you have bathed today, it is true relative to the context, since you have sufficient justification (you're not delusional, you remember correctly since your memory is working fine) to count as knowing. The argument above is not a sound one in this context since the conclusion that you don't have knowledge of the external world is false because you do know that you bathed today. But note that there's no real disagreement between you and the sceptic since it can be true that you don't know you bathed today relative to the sceptic's context and true that you do know relative to an ordinary context.

Note that this isn't really a full-blown solution to the sceptical problem. The contextualist doesn't say that the sceptic's argument is always wrong. Unlike the previous solutions, it's not trying to say how the argument goes wrong, for instance, by saying that Premise 2 is wrong because of inference to the best explanation. What it says is that just because the argument works in the sceptic's context, it doesn't mean it works every time. It is actually true that we know in these other contexts, and we doubt that we know because we mistakenly think that the sense of the verb 'know' is the same in every context when it isn't. But more importantly, the contextualist also explains why we find the sceptic's argument plausible in some contexts and implausible in others.

One objection that the philosopher Earl Conee[xiv] makes is that the standard for the truth of what counts as knowledge is unvarying and actually quite high, but when people ordinarily say someone has knowledge on standards that vary in contexts, it's just loose talk. In fact, fluent speakers of a language do understand that when they ascribe knowledge to someone in a low standard context, they're just talking loosely. The moment we ask Keith DeRose in Bank case A if he *really and truly* knows, he might actually doubt it. This shows that all along, the standard for saying he knows is high and unvarying. Conee says that only when we're perceiving something really clearly, or we have clear memories, or we have triple-checked, do we pass the 'really and truly' test. I leave my house thinking I know I have locked the door, but a minute later when my wife asks me whether I really and truly know that I locked it, I don't know because I go and check again if I have locked it.

Conee says that the contextualist might reply to this that it's just that the standards were raised when the 'really and truly' question was asked, so I do know when the standard is low earlier. But then we have the same results in the 'really or truly' test with respect to a lot of other questions. People start doubting their casual attributions of happiness or friendship or value of some goal when they're asked if they are really and truly happy or who are really and truly their friends and if what they're pursuing is really and truly worth it. However, when it comes to these issues, it looks more plausible to say that we're stopping our casual talk. The contextualist says words like 'happiness' and 'friendship' have contextually varying standards. The contextualist would say that the person who says that before being asked the 'really and truly' question for happiness was not actually engaging in loose talk and had the right view of happiness relative to a lower standard. However, it seems wrong to say the person was not engaging in loose talk. It seems correct to say that they were actually engaging in casual talk, and it's okay to doubt that they weren't really and truly happy or friends or doing something worthwhile.

The Relevant Alternatives Theory

Let's look at another theory that attempts to deal with the sceptical problem. Consider the first premise of the sceptic's argument:

Premise 1: If you have knowledge of the external world, then know that you are not a brain-in-a-vat (BIV).

This is a result of a principle for knowledge known as the closure principle:

If S knows that p, and S knows that p entails q, then S knows that q.

Suppose you know that there is a snake in front of you. That it is a snake entails that it is not a rope, and suppose you know this. If you know that there is a snake in front of you entails that the snake is not a rope, then you know that the snake in front of you is not a rope. And note that suppose you're seeing something snake-like from a distance. However, you haven't ruled out that it's a rope. As a result, since you don't know that the snake in front of you is not a rope, then you don't know it's a snake.

Similarly, you know that what is in front of you is a snake. That it is a snake entails that you're not undergoing an experience given to you as a BIV. If you know this, then you know that you're not undergoing an experience given to you as a BIV. This is an instance of Premise 1, where your knowing that there is a snake in front of you is an instance of knowledge of the external world. So you can see how the closure principle motivates Premise 1.

But one way of dealing with the sceptical problem is to deny

Premise 1 by arguing that you can have knowledge of the external world even though you don't know that you are not a brain-in-a-vat.

Fred Dretske[xv] famously gives the following case:

Zebra Case: You go with your son to a zoo. You see many zebras and tell your son that they are zebras. First question: Do you know they are zebras? Yes, because you know how zebras look, you're in a zoo, and they're in a pen marked 'Zebras'. Second question: Do you know they're not mules cleverly painted by the zoo authorities to make them seem like zebras? Well, since you haven't examined them thoroughly or double-checked with the zoo authorities, your evidence for them being zebras has been undermined because the evidence doesn't show that they're not mules disguised a zebras. That's why you don't know that they're not mules cleverly disguised as zebras. You might even say that it's not likely or wonder what reason the zoo authorities might have for doing so. But what matters isn't what's likely or plausible but the mere possibility, and the fact that you haven't eliminated it yet, shows that the hypothesis that they are mules disguised as zebras hasn't been shown to be false. It might still be possible that they are zebras. Thus, you don't know that they are not mules disguised as zebras.

What Dretske says is that he agrees with the sceptic when it comes to the answer to the second question – that you don't know that they're not mules disguised as zebras. But he says that, unlike the sceptic, he knows that they are zebras. This in effect denies the closure principle (if S knows that p, and S knows that p entails q, then S knows that q). Because you can know that p (in this case that the animals in the zoo are zebras) and know that p entails q (in this case that they are not mules disguised as zebras) and yet do not know that q (that they are not mules disguised as zebras).

Why does he think that? His explanation looks at an analogy

with statements involving explanations. Suppose you were to explain why Brenda did not have any dessert even though it was a part of the meal. You explain this by saying she was full. But what you're explaining is not merely the isolated fact that Brenda did not have any dessert but why Brenda did not have any dessert *rather* than ordering dessert and eating it. If you change this contrast to Brenda did not have any dessert *rather* than ordering dessert and throwing it at the waiter, it's very strange if you explain this by saying because she was full. You not only have to now change the explanation (that she was full) but even what is being explained changes. You're no longer explaining the same thing.

So Dretske says that the fact that Brenda did not have any dessert has to be put in an explanatory context, which involves a network of related facts that are called relevant alternatives. These relevant alternatives are what might have taken place if what actually happened hadn't occurred. The relevant alternative for Brenda not having dessert is her taking the dessert and eating it, for which the explanation is that she was full. It is this possibility that determines what is being explained.

As per Dretske, these relevant alternatives also occur with statements that involve knowledge. You know p only within the network of relevant alternatives q, and s. Just like how relevant alternatives determine what is being explained in the case of explanations, they also define what is known when someone knows that p. Suppose S knows that Lefty killed Otto. If you put the emphasis on Lefty in *Lefty* killed Otto, S knows that it was Lefty who killed *rather* than George, Mike or another suspect. But if you have the emphasis on killed in Lefty *killed* Otto, then S knows that Lefty killed Otto *rather* than injured him or threatened him. That's why, if you change the relevant set of contrasts, what is known changes.

That's why the theory is called the Relevant Alternatives Theory or Epistemic Contrastivism: to know that p, all you need to do is rule out only the relevant alternatives to p. Knowledge for Dretske is a contrastive state, and a complete description of knowledge is not just S knows that p but S knows rather p *rather than* q. How does this deal with scepticism?

If we look at the zebra case, you know that it's a zebra rather than a giraffe. It being a giraffe is a relevant alternative since this is close to reality because it has a high chance of being true. For Dretske, what makes an alternative relevant are the facts in the environment of the subject, even if the person is not aware of them.

Still, given the possibility of there being cleverly disguised mules, you don't know that it's not a cleverly disguised mule. Note, however, that if there's a high chance of it being true that it's a cleverly disguised mule, given that zookeepers in this area tend to do that sort of thing, then this alternative becomes relevant, and you don't know that it's a zebra rather than a cleverly disguised mule. Still, as long as the possibility of there being a cleverly disguised mule isn't relevant, you know that it's a zebra rather than a giraffe even though you don't know that it's a cleverly disguised mule (because you haven't ruled out the possibility). That's how Dretske denies the closure principle (If S knows that p, and S knows that p entails q, then S knows that q.). You can know that p and yet not know that q even though you know that p entails q.

By denying closure, Dretske deals with scepticism because the scenarios the sceptic gives are not relevant as they are too far-fetched. You can thus know that you have hands and yet not know that you are not a brain-in-a-vat because you know you have hands *rather than* not have hands, where not having hands is the relevant alternative. So Premise 1 (if you have knowledge of the external world, then know that you are not a brain-in-a-vat) is false, which shows that the sceptic's argument is unsound.

Keith Derose's objection to rejecting closure is that if we reject it, we are forced to say something implausible like, 'While he doesn't know he's not a bodiless and handless brain-in-a-vat, still, he knows he has hands.' He calls this the abominable conjunction.

Experimental Philosophy and the Zebra Case

In a study, Krzysztof Sękowski, Adrian Ziółkowski and Maciej Tarnowski gave the following case to participants:

> Mike is a young man visiting the zoo with his son, and when they come to the zebra cage, Mike points to the animal and says, 'That's a zebra.' Mike is right – it is a zebra. However, as the older people in his community know, there are lots of ways that people can be tricked into believing things that aren't true. Indeed, the older people in the community know that it's possible that zoo authorities could cleverly disguise mules to look just like zebras, and people viewing the animals would not be able to tell the difference. If the animal that Mike called a zebra had really been such a cleverly painted mule, Mike still would have thought that it was a zebra. Does Mike really know that the animal is a zebra, or does he only believe that it is?[xvi]

Out of 415 participants (204 Indians and 211 Westerners from the US), 55.9 per cent of Indians responded that Mike knows it is a zebra but only 41.7 per cent of Westerners said that Mike knew.

Now what is interesting is the explanation they had for this difference (it's an interesting but tentative one since even though the differences are significant, they aren't that great). Their explanation was that sceptical themes were more influential in Western philosophy and culture whereas even though sceptical themes were present in Indian philosophy, realist themes were way more prevalent. The sceptical themes since ancient times bring into question the mechanisms by which we gain knowledge (like perception, analogy or testimony) and particularly perception.

In Western popular culture, we can see these in movies like *The Matrix*, *Inception* and *The Truman Show* that question the reliability of perception as a way of gaining knowledge. For instance, in *The Matrix*, the main character, Neo, is a computer hacker who finds out that supercomputers have put humans into a vat with nutrients, feeding them their experiences and using them as a source of power. So reality as experienced is artificial, and as a result, Neo rebels against the supercomputers.

On the other hand, the Nyāya school of philosophy in India, which was one of the main schools of philosophy in the Classical era (there were six orthodox schools that recognized the authority of the Vedas, called the Āstika schools, and three Nāstika schools that rejected the authority of the Vedas) held that four means of knowledge are legitimate: *pratyakṣa* (perception), *anumāṇa* (inference), *upamāna* (comparison and analogy) and *śabda* (word, testimony of past or present reliable experts). Even the most sceptical school, which was radically materialist, called the Cārvāka school, took sense perception to be the only legitimate means of knowledge. And even though there were sceptical arguments made by Jayarāśi in the eighth and ninth centuries, they were criticized very widely and didn't pose a threat to the prevalent views.

The Nyāya school has a very interesting response to dream scepticism, which is like external world scepticism. In fact, in his *Meditations,* Descartes gave the argument for it right before he gave the demon argument. He writes:

> How often have I dreamt that I was in these familiar circumstances, that I was dressed, and occupied this

> place by the fire, when I was lying undressed in bed? At the present moment, however, I certainly look upon this paper with eyes wide awake; the head which I now move is not asleep; I extend this hand consciously and with express purpose, and I perceive it; the occurrences in sleep are not so distinct as all this. But I cannot forget that, at other times I have been deceived in sleep by similar illusions; and, attentively considering those cases, I perceive so clearly that there exist no certain marks by which the state of waking can ever be distinguished from sleep, that I feel greatly astonished; and in amazement I almost persuade myself that I am now dreaming.[xvii]

Descartes basically argues that there is no way to distinguish a dream from a waking experience. That's why I can't know whether I am dreaming or not. The argument is almost identical to the demon argument.

Premise 1: If you have knowledge of the external world, then you know that you are not dreaming.

Premise 2: You don't know you aren't dreaming.

Conclusion: You don't have knowledge of the external world.

Very interestingly Vātsyāyana, in his commentary on the *Nyāya Sutra*,[xviii] shows the argument that the opponents of the Nyāya view that perception is a reliable means of knowledge that shows things as they are:

> The opponent argues that beliefs about sources of knowledge and known objects are false like false beliefs in a dream and are not like perception of objects in waking; there is no proof here… there is also no proof that objects presented in a dream are unreal.

> Objection: (dream objects are unreal) because of not being perceived while awake.
>
> Reply: ... If being perceived shows existence, non-perception may show non-existence; but if there is non-existence in both cases, lack of perception would not have the ability (to show non-existence).[xix]

The passage from Descartes reminds one starkly of this passage. The argument of Nyāya's opponent here is that there is no evidence that distinguishes the objects in waking from those in a dream. We can't therefore say that the objects we experience while waking are real or that the objects in a dream are unreal either. One may reply to this that the reason they are unreal is because we don't perceive them in our waking moments. But the opponent's response is to say that this merely begs the question, that is, the response assumes that what we perceive when we are awake is real. But it's still possible that they are unreal, and if they were, then we would not be able to differentiate them from those in a dream.

The Nyāya response to this is fascinating. Consider our memories and desires. All our memories and desires are about what has been experienced before. That is, if I have a memory, it is of something experienced before, and if I have a desire, it is of something I have experienced before. Of course, we can have false memories and desires that are about unreal things, but even then, the objects of the memories and desires will contain some element of a previous experience. Since memories and desires are grounded in a past experience, you can't show that the past experience is false based on the memory. Rather, it's the other way around. It is only on the basis of past experiences that we can say that a memory is fake and a desire is delusional. There is an asymmetry between that which is grounded (the memory or the desire) and the ground itself (the experience).

Our dreams are like memories and desires. They, too, are

grounded in past experiences. Either the dream has nothing in common with past experience or it has. But there is no evidence that dreams don't have anything in common with previous experiences. And if there is evidence that there is something in common with past experience, then dreams do not provide a ground for showing the past experience to be false (a better word would be non-veridical instead of false). For the Nyāya view, if both dreams and experiences are symmetrical, that is, if they are both false, the dreams should also be able to provide grounds for showing the experience to be false, but that's not possible.

The Nyāya Sutra says, 'And false beliefs in a dream are like memory and desire (for what has been experienced before).'[xx]

In his commentary on this, Vātsyāyana says, 'Just as memory and desire have as their contents something experienced before and cannot set that aside, so also objects in dreams are taken from what is experienced before and cannot set that aside.'[xxi]

He says that you can't mistake a stump for a person if you haven't seen a person. Having seen a person is the root experience of your mistaking a stump for a person. Likewise, having a dream experience in which you claim that you see an elephant is grounded in the root experience of you having experienced an elephant. If the root experience of the person itself was an error, the error was because that had another root experience. If that other root experience was an error, then that had a root experience... you can see where this is going. You need to have non-erroneous root experiences in order to stop this infinite regress. That's why scepticism is wrong.

Now try to apply this to Descartes' demon argument and the brain-in-a-vat argument and see whether it begs the question or not. Sweet dreams!

PERSONAL IDENTITY

Imagine there is a machine, called a Teletransporter, that can copy all states of your cells in your body with 100 per cent accuracy and send them all to Mars. That way, you'll be on Mars at the speed of light. Another machine on Mars, the Replicator, will recreate your body and brain exactly the same as before. The only catch is, that if you decide to go into the Teletransporter and press the right button, you can only be on Mars if your current brain and body are completely destroyed. Would you press the button?

Your answer depends on whether you believe that that new person would be the same person as you. If you believe it isn't, and that by pressing the button, you'll be destroyed, you don't believe that that person is the same person as you. Notice one thing, though. In this case, the new person on Mars is *qualitatively identical* to you, in that it has the same properties you have, but it's *not numerically identical* to you. It's not *one and the same* person as you. Keep this distinction in mind. If you make a duplicate of a key, then the duplicate is qualitatively identical but not numerically identical to the original key. But the original key is one and the same key as what it was before the duplication. It is numerically identical to what it was.

Now if you believe that the new person is the same person as you before pressing the button, then the new person is numerically identical to you. There's another catch with the belief that the Mars person is the same person as you. Due to a malfunction in the Teletransporter, suppose your cells don't get destroyed, but the Replicator still recreates you on Mars. You're still there on Earth. But because you're in violation of the Proliferation of Person's Act (a law that happens to be in place in this imaginary scenario) because there's more than one of you, the original you has to be killed. If you're one of those who said that you and the one on Mars are the same person, you're in a fix because most likely, the original you wouldn't want to die.[i] But note that this isn't very different from your cells being destroyed utterly. So maybe you'll have to say it's not the same person on Mars. We'll look at this issue in a bit more detail later.

The Problem of Personal Identity

Given that there are two sorts of responses to the Teletransporter case, this question arises: What makes a person the same person over time, that is numerically identical over time? You look at yourself ten years from now and ask: What makes me the same person as that one over time? This is the philosophical question about personal identity, and philosophers look for criteria for personal identity. The question becomes more significant since, in our lifetimes, every cell in our body is gradually changed and completely replaced. But there has to be something common that persists through change. The problem is, what makes this the same over time?

But there is another question similar to this. People often ask themselves the question, 'Who am I?' This question is different from the philosophical question since it looks at how you see yourself or what traits make you unique. So don't get confused, because this isn't what is at stake here.

The fact that we are numerically identical over time forms the basis of holding people responsible and making plans for our future. You can't hold a person responsible for murder if that person isn't the same person as the one who committed it. You make plans for your retirement because the future self is the same as you. So this is an important question. But what is the criterion of personal identity?

Before we go on, it's not as simple as saying having the same DNA is the criterion for personal identity. Since a person can have the same DNA as a clone and yet be a different person. So no. That's a no-starter.

The Psychological Criterion

If you think that you and the person on Mars are the same person, then you might think it's because the person on Mars shares your consciousness. This becomes clearer in a thought experiment by John Locke.[ii]

The Prince and the Cobbler: The consciousness of a cobbler gets transferred to a prince's body and that of the prince goes to the cobbler's body. Would the person in the cobbler's body be the prince and the one in the prince's body be the cobbler?

It looks like because the cobbler has the prince's consciousness and memories, the person in the cobbler's body is the prince and the person in the prince's body is the cobbler. So it is consciousness that is responsible for what makes a person the same across time. In this case, for Locke, consciousness extends backwards to previous thoughts and actions through memory. On that basis, Locke's theory (at least on one interpretation) is called the naïve memory theory and is thus: (Let x be a person at an earlier time and y be a person at a later time.)

x at time t_1 is the same as y at time t_2 if and only if y remembers x's experiences.

Note that if y remembers x's experiences, then y remembers from the inside, so to speak, rather than remembering someone else's actions as a spectator. So that's why it seems intuitive that this makes a person the same person rather than another person.

But there's an objection to this, given by the philosopher Thomas Reid in the eighteenth century.[iii] Suppose there's a boy who was punished at school for having stolen from an orchard (let the boy be x). That boy grows up to be a soldier (who is y) who takes the enemy's flag the first time he goes to war. When he grows older, he becomes a general (let the general be z). The soldier remembers the punishment as a boy. The general doesn't remember the punishment as a boy but remembers his youth as a soldier taking the flag.

If x is identical to y so long as x remembers y's experiences, the soldier is identical to the boy, and the general is identical to the soldier. But strangely, the general isn't identical to the boy because he doesn't remember his experience. This violates the law of transitivity of identity, which is relevant to identity. This law states that if $x = y$, and $y = z$, then $x = z$. For instance, if $2+2 = 4$ and $3+1 = 4$, then $2+2 = 3+1$. But in the case of the boy, soldier and the general, $x = y$, $y = z$ but $x \neq z$. Which is wrong.

One way to deal with this problem is to say that there is an unbroken chain of memories connecting each person stage. A person stage is just a person at a particular time, like a person as a baby, a person as a teenager etc. Let's call this the Stream Theory. Suppose x is the stage of a person, and y is another stage and z is the end point of a series of stages. Z is connected to each previous person stage in the series via a memory to y and so on all the way back to x. What this means is that the general remembers what he did five minutes back, this person stage remembers what he did a month back, which remembers what the soldier did, and the soldier remembers what the child did. As long as there is this continuity in memory, even though the general doesn't remember what the child did, personal identity is still preserved.[iv]

Of course, there's an objection to this, too. Suppose Sita has an accident and gets total amnesia. Every memory is wiped out. It's still the same person. If that is so, even though there is a break in the chain of memories connecting her with her past person stages, this person is identical to the Sita before the accident. Now, it's not just that Sita has lost memory of events; she has also lost factual memory, that is the memory that the earth goes around the sun, as well as the memory of how to do things like drive. But if we go by the Stream Theory, the break in the continuity of memory, shows that the amnesiac Sita after the accident isn't the same person as the one before it. On the other hand, it seems clear that she is.

This gets even weirder if Sita regains her memories. Because as we just saw on the Stream Theory, Sita with amnesia is not identical to Sita before amnesia. And therefore, Sita after she regains the memories is not identical to Sita before amnesia, since the continuity of memories is broken. Which leads to the strange conclusion that Sita didn't survive the accident and there's someone different who regained memories!

One way of revising this theory is by Sydney Shoemaker. He says that personal identity will be preserved so long as the person's personality, interests, tastes, character and personality are preserved. As a result, there is general psychological continuity rather than just memory continuity. One might reply that Sita then might have the same personality, tastes, etc., as another person, but that doesn't mean that she is identical to that person. But on Shoemaker's view, it's not just that Sita after the amnesia has the same traits as Sita before the amnesia, but that she has them because Sita's life before amnesia was the life through which she gained those traits.

This, too, leads to a problem with the Teletransporter case. As we saw, suppose the Teletransporter malfunctions and your original body doesn't get destroyed on Earth. The Replicator on Mars has created a person who is psychologically continuous with you. Let the original you be x, the one that remains on Earth after Teletransportation be y and the person on Mars be z. Then with the psychological continuity view, there's a violation of transitivity. Because x=y, x=z but y ≠ z.

Fission Cases

Suppose your brain were to be transplanted into another person's body. It looks clear that since the character and memories are the same, the person in the new body is you. Now imagine that half your brain gets transferred to a body with an empty head and the other half gets destroyed. You can still survive that transplant. When the corpus callosum that connects the two hemispheres of the brain is removed, each half of the brain still functions. It's therefore plausible that if half of that is transplanted, the person survives. The person in the new body will still be you.

Lefty and Righty: The left hemisphere of your brain goes to a new body, and the right hemisphere goes to another body. Both the new bodies had heads that were previously empty. The body with the left hemisphere of your brain is Lefty and the one with the right is Righty. Which one of them is you?

Based on what we saw with the transplant when one half gets transplanted and the other half destroyed, if you can survive with half a brain destroyed, there's no reason why you can't survive with the other half of your brain intact.

But this leads us back to the same problem we saw with the malfunctioning Teletransporter. Let's say the original you with both hemispheres intact is x, Lefty is y and Righty is z. Then x = y, x = z but y ≠ z.

One response to this sort of problem is by Shoemaker. He says that you are identical to the person if half your brain is transplanted as long as there is no branching. This means that the original person is identical to the one with half the hemisphere so long as the other hemisphere is destroyed (if it wasn't destroyed, that'll be the branch coming out, so that's why there's no branching). It sounds really clever. That way, you don't get the violation of transitivity because there is no z that y is not identical to. This is called the non-branching condition. So long as there is no z existing simultaneously with y that is psychologically continuous with x, x is identical to y. If there is another z, then the original you ceases to exist, since you aren't identical with either y or z.

You can see the non-branching condition with the Teletransporter case, too. If the Teletransporter doesn't malfunction, the person on Mars is identical to you. If it does malfunction, the original you *before* the button was pressed in the Transporter isn't identical to the you that remains on Earth *after* the button is pressed because branching has taken place. You have just died!

Notice that logically, this is quite airtight and neat. Yet it leads to the bizarre conclusion that if Righty exists alongside Lefty, then the original you just died! The reason why it's strange is because it makes a fact of Lefty's identity dependent on something outside of it, which is really weird. The non-branching condition is also wild since it seems that you survive with half the brain, but with more of the brain, you don't. Surely, more is better when it comes to survival.

One clever way out of this is by Derek Parfit.[v] He says that you survive as both Lefty and Righty but are not identical to them. This simply means that in the case of Lefty and Righty, you *survive* as both people but are not *identical* to them. How is that even possible?

We already know why you are not identical to them. Because identity is a logically one–one relation. If you are identical to someone, then transitivity holds, that is, x=y and y=z, then x=z. There can only be one but not two of you. So you can't be identical to either Lefty or Righty. But what Parfit says is that this lack of personal identity in the branching case doesn't really matter. Why? Because if it did matter to us, it would be death. But as mentioned above, if you survive with half a brain, how can a scenario that is even more successful, in which both your hemispheres survive, be death?

What Parfit says is this. Parfit accepts the non-branching criterion for personal identity, that so long as there is no z existing simultaneously with y that is psychologically continuous with x, x is identical to y. But in the branching case, there's no answer to the question 'Is this the same person as me?' Yet I still survive, because survival isn't a logically one–one relation but comes as a matter of degree. Memories get weak, and they fade, and the stage of me that I have more memories of, I am more psychologically connected to that. So more of that part of me survives. Plus it's not logically one–one because x remembers y, y remembers z, but x may not remember z, and yet there can be overlapping chains of psychological continuity.

What really matters to me in survival is that the person in the future has my memories and carries out my intentions, not that the person is the same as me. This is just like an example Parfit gives. The French Socialist Party split in 1881, but asking whether the French Socialist Party stopped existing or is one and the same as one of the parties is just an empty question. Similarly, asking whether I am the same person as Lefty or Righty is an empty question.

The Circularity Objection

But wait. It still can't be right. Say that I survived the Teletransporter on Mars even though my body was destroyed. I definitely don't want to be killed on Earth if the Teletransporter malfunctions and my body is still here. There has to be a stronger objection to Parfit.

Let's look at what a circular argument is first. A person makes the argument that I should believe in God because the Bible says so. But If I ask him why I should believe in the Bible, the person says because God says so. We come full circle because if you ask him again why you should believe in God, he'll go on to say the Bible says so, and it'll go on that way. The argument is circular because the claim that the person is trying to show to be true is already assumed in the premise. The claim in question is whether God exists but the argument already assumes that God exists. In effect, God exists because God exists.

Now the circularity objection to Locke's memory criterion was one given by Bishop Joseph Butler in the eighteenth century.[vi] Suppose I am Napoleon and I have a memory of winning the battle of Waterloo. It is *my* memory. There's also a madman who claims to have the same memory. But the memories can be distinguished only because the former is my memory and the latter is a false memory. To distinguish the two, the genuine memory is only a genuine one because the memory is of the person identical to the same person who had the experience.

Look what happens now. The memory criterion for identity says that x is identical to y so long as x remembers y's experience. But the memory is a genuine memory of y's experience precisely because x is identical to y. You can't appeal to memory to say that x is identical to y because, for the memory to be a genuine memory, x has to be identical to y. We end up with a circularity. You tried to explain personal identity by appealing to facts about memory. But that fact about memory itself rests on a fact about personal identity. You can't appeal to memory to define personal identity because the requisite memory assumes personal identity.

Parfit, the clever guy that he was, tried to get around this by talking about quasi-memories, or Q-memories. It's like a magic trick. He's like okay you can define memories without appealing to personal identity. How?

In the movie *Total Recall* with Arnold Schwarzenegger, there's a company that implants memories into people to make them experience things in their memories without having actually done them.[vii] You can enjoy the memory of having a holiday at the beach through this implanted memory. In fact, you can even have another person's real memories and they can be implanted into you. So you have these apparent memories. You get so addicted to these memory implants, and after a while, you can't distinguish between a genuine memory and the implanted one. You have to work out which apparent memory is yours or implanted. When you see a memory you guess is yours, you say, 'Someone, probably I, had the experience.' But it doesn't necessarily mean that it is yours since it might be implanted. You have these apparent memories, which Parfit calls Q-memories (quasi-memories), some of which are yours and some implanted.

You can see the trick he did here. One can define these q-memories without reference to them being yours since they might be implanted. Having a q-memory doesn't imply that it's yours, so you can define personal identity just with reference to q-memories. For Parfit, psychological continuity then consists of the continuity of q-memories, q-beliefs, q-intentions, etc. A subject S q-remembers an experience if

1. S has a belief about a past experience that seems in itself like a memory belief.

2. Someone did have such an experience.

3. S's belief is dependent upon this experience in the same way (whatever it is)

This doesn't assume the continued existence of a person. This frees memory from an assumption of personal identity. Clever!

But Marya Schechtman has an amazing objection to this.[viii] Consider the following cases:

Jane and Paul: Jane has undergone a memory implant, and she has Paul's memories. A storm in Venice and a streak of lightning over the San Giorgio bell tower is particularly vivid in her memory, despite not having gone to Venice. She finds out that Paul actually had an experience of these things. As per Parfit, this isn't a delusion because it is an accurate q-memory and Jane knows it is of Paul's experiences.

Small Change: A philosopher named Edward Casey recounts (not a fictional case) going on a family outing to watch a movie called *Small Change*. He has his wife and two children with him, eats at a restaurant called Clark's, goes to a bookstore and then goes to watch the movie. At the movie, he has specific emotional responses to it and glances at the subtitles when he can't understand the movie, which is in French.

Schechtman then hypothesizes that Casey's memory of the outing is implanted in Jane. A dilemma arises. Either Jane experiences the visual content of Casey's memory and doesn't interpret it the way Casey does, or she has the same memory with all the personal responses and associations involved in it.

If Jane merely experiences the visual content without interpreting it like Casey, then the quasi-memory won't capture what is relevant in the memory to personal identity compared to what happens when we look at genuine memories. Because it misses out on all the personal elements, like it being an outing with 'my' family, as it appears for Casey. If it is just a series of images for Jane, then it's not qualitatively even the same memory as Casey's. Not only that, since Jane doesn't know things associated with Casey's home town, as in what is what, it'll just appear as a blur of sounds and images that can't be identified. Not only is it not a quasi-memory of a family outing, but it's not a memory either, since that's not how memories are.

So if you remove personal elements from the memory, you end up in trouble. If you only retain the visual content without the original experiencer's interpretation, then it's either not the same memory that is implanted or not a memory at all. To identify the memory as that memory, you have to say it is Casey's memory, which assumes personal identity.

Now let's look at the second part of the dilemma. Jane experiences the memory with all its personal elements. On Parfit's view, Jane should be able to separate the personal aspects from the visual content when she reflects on it. So, she doesn't think of the family as her family, like in Casey's memory, but thinks the family isn't hers but whosever's memory it is. But then Schechtman says that even then her quasi-memory isn't qualitatively identical to Casey's memory. If Jane experiences the memory with personal associations, she'll be shocked and confused to experience Casey's family as her family. She would think of it as a delusion, as not being part of her coherent life story. Even if we could reproduce the memory exactly by suppressing Jane's feelings like this is not her family, then it'll be a delusion since it will appear as her family.

Recall Butler's circularity objection. It said that to distinguish the madman and Napoleon's actual memory, you'll have to appeal to personal identity. The reason Napoleon's memory is genuine is because it was his memory, but the madman's wasn't. Parfit tried to say that you can define memory as q-memory without appealing to personal identity and then differentiate between Napoleon's memory and the madman's by saying that the former is psychologically connected with an experience and the latter isn't. But in the case of Jane, she ends up with a memory that is deluded even though it is a q-memory that is psychologically connected to an experience. We go back to the circle again. Parfit can't distinguish between a delusional case and a non-delusional one by using q-memories because one would be deluded if one had another person's q-memories. To show it's not deluded, he'll have to end up saying that the memory is genuine because it is the same person's memory. If he assumes that it is Jane's memory, only then can he say it isn't deluded.

What Schechtman's argument against Parfit shows is that if you take Casey's memory and implant it in Jane, you can't separate the identity of the person and whose memory it is from the memory itself. Thus, you can't define a memory without reference to personal identity, and the circularity objection still stands.

Physical Criteria

So maybe there's a problem with psychological criteria of personal identity. Perhaps we need to look at physical criteria as opposed to mental criteria. Psychological criteria of personal identity involved mental states, which are private, like beliefs, memories and desires, that cannot be observed publicly. Maybe the answer in the relation between physical states, that are publicly observable states like states of the body or the brain.

Let's get back to the Teletransporter case. You might think that the person on Mars is not you and that when your cells are destroyed on Earth after the Teletransportation, you die. That's why, you might think that because it's not your body that's on Mars and that the destruction of your body entails your destruction, it might be plausible to think that you are your body. So:

x at time t_1 is the same as y at time t_2 if and only if y has the same body as x.

Why might this be plausible?

One reason is that even though every cell of your body gets replaced over time, your body is the same body, and this is what persists. And you persist because you are that body that remains constant over time. Plus, a lot of us think that once our body dies, we die. *The end of the body is the end of me, so I must be my body and past me and present me if I have the same body. It is my body that is conscious and capable of rationality, so the I must be my body.* There's a very interesting thought experiment by Bernard Williams[ix] to show that bodily continuity is the criterion for personal identity.

Suppose someone, say an evil scientist, tells me that the next day I'll be physically tortured. But before being tortured, my brain will be zapped so I have total amnesia during the course of my being tortured. Should I be afraid of this torture?

It looks like amnesia wouldn't comfort me, and I'll still be afraid. Because I can think of it like being in an accident and waking up with memory loss and still being in massive pain. At least here, it looks like the psychological continuity theory is wrong because my intuition is that since it is me who will be tortured, I am afraid. What then matters to personal identity is that the body is continuous.

Now imagine that not only are all your memories removed but your character is changed, too, and illusory memories that don't belong to anyone else that make me think I'm King George IV are added also. Even if the memories are memories that are the same as that of another person who's currently alive, this isn't comforting either. Just because there happens to be another person B on whom my memories are modelled, it doesn't make any difference between this and there being illusory memories. Plus, not only will I be tortured, but there'll be madness, too.

Let's look at something like Locke's memory swap case of the prince and the cobbler. Suppose there's another person B whose memories have get copied into my brain before the torture. The psychological continuity theorist might say that because the memories in the body to be tortured have been caused by B's experiences, the person to be tortured is B. Because it is psychologically connected with B's experiences, the body is thus B, and I shouldn't be afraid that the body will be tortured. But Williams looks at the analogy of character. What difference does it make if the change in the character of the body to be tortured is modelled on B or is caused by B's experiences? I'll still fear pain. Similarly, what difference does it make if the memories are modelled on B in the previous case or if they are caused by B's experiences? And even if your current memories were to be transferred to B, exactly like in the prince and the cobbler case, this shouldn't make a difference either. Because something happening to someone else shouldn't determine what you are. Thus, I fear torture in all these cases because the body that will be tortured is me.

The problem with this argument is that suppose it was another brain being transplanted into my body and my brain gets destroyed.[x] It looks like if I identified with my body, the body still remains, but since the brain isn't mine, it's not me in the new body but the person whose brain it is. In this case, what I'll fear isn't torture but death. Analogously, when all my psychological states are zapped, what I fear isn't torture but my death. Of course, given that we've seen major problems with psychological continuity theories, one can just claim that I am my brain. Thus:

x at time t_1 is the same as y at time t_2 if and only if x and y have the same brain.

But suppose your brain is gradually replaced by silicon parts, given advances in tech. It can still function.[xi] If it is replaced fully by silicon parts to the extent that it is now fully silicon, it's no longer the brain, but you still persist. It's no longer the brain because the brain is, by its very nature, a biological entity like the heart or liver. The function can be substituted by the silicon brain, but it's not the same brain because the previous one was biological and this isn't. Thus, you can still persist without the same brain, so the brain criterion is false.

Animalism

Another physical criterion is given by a view called Animalism.

The view holds that we are human animals, that is, I am identical to a human animal. This is not the same as saying that a person is identical to the matter that makes up a human animal. On the face of it, why would someone adhere to animalism? Because if the human animal isn't identical to me, it might be something that isn't me, and it is strange to say that. So:

x at time t_1 is the same as y at time t_2 if and only if x and y are the same human animal.

This means that you persist so long as your metabolism, and other biological functions like the capacity for blood circulation, continue. Note that being an animal isn't sufficient for being a person. There can be an animal without it being a person, like a toad, since it isn't rational, intelligent and self-conscious. But even all human animals aren't people since a human in a permanent vegetative state might be alive but isn't a person because of the loss of mental capacities. Being an animal isn't necessary for being a person either since, in principle, there can be gods or angels who are persons without being animals.

The claim that animalism makes is that all human persons are animals. If you are a human person, then you're an animal. For animalism, if your brain is transplanted into another body, that becomes a new animal and ceases to be you. Because that's a different biological organism.

Animalism isn't the same view as the bodily continuity view. This is because if you replace inorganic parts with parts of your body, only the organic parts can be called the animal.[xii] The animal just gets smaller and smaller as its organic parts are replaced by inorganic ones. The idea is that if your body becomes fully inorganic, you're still your body but you're not an animal. That's why it's not the same view.

One major argument for animalism, called the Thinking-Animal Argument, given by Eric Olson,[xiii] goes like this:

Premise 1. There is a human animal sitting on your chair.

Premise 2. The human animal sitting on your chair is thinking.

Premise 3. The thinking being sitting on your chair is you.

Conclusion. You are the human animal sitting on your chair.

Olson argues that it is tough to deny any of these premises.

Suppose one were to deny Premise 1 and claim that there is no human animal sitting on your chair. You might claim that is no human animal because there aren't any human animals. And if there aren't any human animals, there's no reason why there should be other kinds of organisms either. It's bizarre to deny that there are any other organisms.

Denying the second premise – 'the human animal sitting on your chair is thinking' – would mean that you'll have to say that the human animal isn't thinking. This is also strange because if the human animal with a functioning mature brain can't think, then not only can no human animal think, but animals with lesser developed brains can't think either.

Perhaps one can deny the third premise – that you are the thinking being sitting on your chair. Since one can't just say that you're not the thinking being by saying that you don't exist, one might say that there's another thinker apart from the animal, and that's the actual you. So there's more than one thinker on your chair – the thinking animal, as well as a separate you. There are too many thinkers in the same place! That's a problem indeed.

There's an objection to animalism by Dean Zimmerman,[xiv] which is an objection to premise 1 of the thinking animal argument, which is, that there is a human animal sitting on your chair. Called the rival candidates problem, the objection doesn't say that premise 1 is false, but that it's not enough to show that the conclusion of the argument is true. Why? Because apart from there being a human animal on the chair, it's also the case that there's a 'mere hunk of matter' and 'a mere body' and a 'psychological person' on your chair. And one can just as well say that you are the mere body that's thinking or the hunk of matter that's thinking or the psychological person who's thinking. Which is weird because if you're a psychological person who's thinking, that justifies the psychological continuity view, and if you're a mere body that's thinking, that justifies the bodily continuity view. Unless the animalist comes up with a reason to deny these candidates as thinking entities, the argument doesn't justify the conclusion that you are the thinking animal sitting on the chair.

Personal Identity and Multiple Personality Disorder

Christine Beauchamp (not the real name) was a patient of the neurologist Dr Morton Prince for seven years. This was towards the end of the nineteenth century and the beginning of the twentieth century. In 1893, she was a hospital nurse who underwent three shocks in succession on a stormy night.[xv] She was a nervous, extremely quiet, religious and patient woman who loved books. She went to Dr Prince to get help with her nervousness, fatigue, headaches and depression. Let's call her B I. Dr Prince hypnotized her, so let's call the hypnotic state B Ia. She was the same person as B I but less restrained in the hypnotic state.

Sally: Another personality emerged under hypnotism, who called herself Sally. Sally found B I stupid, couldn't understand French, unlike B I, and had contempt for B I because she wasn't lively and was a bookworm. She also was aware of B I's thoughts, dreams and activities from early childhood. One day, Sally emerged as a separate personality, even in the unhypnotized state, a lively, flirtatious and carefree person, unlike B I. She hated B I so much that she tore her letters and destroyed her sewing and knitting and sent parcels with spiders to her. B I wasn't aware of this and would find herself with a cigarette in her hand even though she didn't smoke.

B IV: Another personality emerged, called B IV. She couldn't recognize Dr Prince and was impatient, very independent, aggressive and hot-tempered. Sally was aware of her actions but not her thoughts. Sally and she were at loggerheads. Sally prevented B IV from sleeping, tired her out and hid her stuff. B IV spoke to herself in French to mislead Sally. B I suddenly started to find an exchange of letters between B IV and Sally and found herself in strange situations with her jobs and friends. B IV's hypnotized version was called B IVa.

B II: B Ia and B IVa combined to form B II. She had the good qualities of both and not their vices. She wasn't aware of Sally, but Sally was aware of her thoughts and actions. B I and B IV felt they were extinct when B II was in charge. Because B I was meek, she accepted this, but because B IV didn't want to be 'squeezed' to being passive by B II, she partnered with Sally to frustrate her, like not going to appointments with Dr Prince so that B II wouldn't come out again under hypnotism. After finishing her autobiography and writing her will, Sally gave up and became extinct voluntarily. B II 'woke up' as Chrstine Beauchamp. Sally went back to being a dormant consciousness, and B II divided into B I, B IV or Sally when under a lot of stress.

The philosopher Kathleen Wilkes does note that perhaps cases like these, called Multiple Personality Disorder, are part of an actual condition or that the condition emerges due to hypnotism. But for the sake of the issue of personal identity, this doesn't matter. She interprets these events as follows.

On the bodily continuity view and animalism, there's only one person since there's only a single body and one animal. But the problem arises because while that might be typically the case with a person to one body (or animal) relation, here there's a one-many relation.

On the psychological continuity view, since B I and B IV said that all of what Beauchamp did before 1893 was what they did, B II not only claimed ownership of Beauchamp's actions before 1893 but also claimed that B I and B IV's behaviour were hers. Therefore, all of them should be identical to each other. The problem is that identity ought to be symmetric, that is, if A = B, then B = A. But in this case, since B I and B IV didn't know of B II's thoughts or actions, B II isn't the same as B I or B IV. Even B I and B IV weren't aware of each other directly, so they're not identical. This faces the problem of transitivity again since B I = B II and B IV = B II but B I ≠ B IV. Plus, Sally isn't identical to any of them because even though she has a memory of everyone else's actions, she didn't remember their actions as her own actions, and they weren't aware of hers.

Even if we add personality traits to the psychological continuity view like Shoemaker did, it turns out that they had very different personalities, tastes and habits, too. In fact, later tests with other multiple personality disorder patients have shown them as having even different allergies.

B I: Bad appetite, preferred unsweetened black coffee, didn't smoke or drink, read religious books, went to church, visited sick people, sewed, knitted, wore loose sober clothes.

B IV: Healthy appetite, coffee with sugar and cream, loved smoking and drinking, read newspapers, bored of church, sick people and sewing and knitting, wore bright, tight clothes.

It looks like they all were different persons. It was also different from the inside as to what it was like to experience things for all of them from the first-person perspective. In fact, for B IV, B II surviving seemed to mean death for her, and it wouldn't have consoled B I or B IV if they were told that they survived as B II. They could be praised and blamed for their behaviour. They were Intentional Systems, too, that is, their behaviour could be predicted based on what they believed and desired.

If Ram believes that it will rain in five minutes and desires to go out but not get wet, we can predict that he will take out his umbrella. This is what it is for one's behaviour to be predicted based on a belief and a desire.

In effect, there seems to be a plurality of persons. But it's very strange to say this because Dr Prince didn't really think of himself as a murderer when he made B I and B IV extinct and Sally to remain permanently in the background as dormant. The problem is, we're left with a plurality of persons on one hand and them not being counted as persons on the other.

To resolve this, Kathleen Wilkes suggests that personal identity is determined by societal norms. For instance, Dr Prince worked with the norm that persons are unitary because of which he tried to extinguish all but one. In fact, various eras have had different ideas of personhood. For instance, the Ancient Greek, view was represented in in Homer's *Iliad*. Homer had characters treated as single individuals, and at the same time, being psychologically or bodily disunited. The individual made decisions in Homer's Iliad, but also by their spirit, their destructive spirit, their heart (their seat of passion), etc. Action could also be initiated by their hands, knees or feet. Basically, there is a single individual who is also a plurality.

In our age, we expect a single, united consciousness to describe a person. But we have cases where this is a disunity of consciousness and yet there is personhood. For instance, there's sleepwalking, there are parts of our selves that don't allow us to do what we want, split brains with two centres of consciousness due to the corpus callosum being removed and where more than our conscious mental experiences, we also have unconscious and non-conscious states. While the unity of consciousness constraint is helpful in judging responsibility based on past actions and intentions in most cases, it doesn't help in complex cases like multiple personality disorder. Wilkes says that we can weaken the unity of consciousness constraint for personhood and see people perhaps as cognitive psychologists do when they see different systems at work in the brain.

The No-Self View

In the case of multiple personalities, even if we think of personal identity as a result of societal norms, we are still left with subjects of experiences that are multiple. And these multiple subjects of experience are not determined by social norms. We can see this in split-brain experiments by Michael Gazzaniga and Roger Sperry.

Gazzaniga and Sperry looked at patients who had their corpus callosum removed.[xvi] The corpus callosum connects two hemispheres of the brain, and it used to be removed to treat epilepsy. Patients were asked to look at the centre of a divided screen, where words and pictures were flashed on each side of the screen. For instance, on the right screen, the picture of a chicken claw was flashed. On the left screen, the picture of a house covered in snow and a snowman in front was flashed. The patients could describe the picture on the right visual field, since speech is in the left hemisphere, but couldn't describe the one on the left. But then, they could select what they had seen from a bag of objects with their left hand. When they were asked to match the pictures, they correctly chose a shovel for the snow with the left hand and selected a chicken with the right hand. Because their hemispheres couldn't communicate, when they were asked why they picked them, they cooked up a story to compensate for ignorance, saying, 'Oh, that's simple. The chicken claw goes with the chicken, and you need a shovel to clean out the chicken shed.'

Perhaps there are two conscious entities in the head or only one. How do we determine how many? One way to deal with the problem is to say that there are two subjects of experience (not based on social norms) like the multiple personality case and yet a single person. This is one option, based on the Ego Theory of the Self, which holds that there is a single entity that is continuous and is what experiences things and acts and makes decisions. The Ego Theory is what we typically tend to hold.

One might, thus, make a distinction between persons and subjects of experiences. The problem with this, which Derek Parfit points out, is that when 'subjects of experience' can exist without being persons, it seems weird to say that they all amount to one person. It at least makes sense to think that a single 'subject of experience' is a single person. But it's a bit incredible to think that there exist two subjects of experience, like in split-brain patients, without being persons.

If there's no way to determine whether there are two entities or one single conscious entity in the case of split-brain patients, this is a problem for the Ego Theory. This sort of problem arises in the first place because of the Ego Theory, which most of us tend to believe. What if the root of all these above issues is that they all assume that there is a persisting self with an essence when, in fact, there is no such thing? The essence of something is what makes something what it is. Essential properties, like water's essence being H_2O, are constant through their changes. In this case, not only does the self not have an essence, but the self doesn't even exist.

David Hume, in his *Treatise of Human Nature* (1739), wrote that, on introspection, he couldn't find the self and thus denied its existence:

> For my part, when I enter most intimately into what I call myself, I always stumble on some particular perception or other, of heat or cold, light or shade, love or hatred, pain or pleasure. I never can catch myself at any time without a perception, and never can observe anything but the perception.[xvii]

In Indian philosophy, too, Buddhists deny the existence of the self. There's a fascinating dialogue in *Milindapañha* (*The*

Questions of King Milinda)[xviii] between the monk Nagasena and King Milinda (or Menander), who was a ruler in northwestern India in the second century BCE. On being asked his name by the king, Nagasena tells the king his name but says that the name is just for practical purposes and doesn't really refer to an individual who is permanent that persists through change. Finding this ridiculous, King Milinda says that if there's no individual that's permanent, then there's no one who provides for monks, no one who meditates, no one who lies or steals and there is no such thing as merit or demerit and no one who will be even murdered if killed! The king asks the monk if Nagasena is identical to any of the five *khandas* or aggregates.[xix] In Buddhist philosophy, the human being is composed of physical form, perceptions, feelings, motives and consciousness. Nagasena replies in the negative. The king says that if Nagasena says he isn't identical to any of the *khandas*, or something else apart from them, then 'Nagasena' is just a sound and what Nagasena has said is false since Nagasena doesn't exist. If we can't refer to anything with the name, not only is there no point in using it, but it's not even a name at all!

In response, Nagasena uses Milinda's reasoning against him by asking him if a chariot is identical with any of its parts: Is it identical with its axle, frame, reins, frame, spoke or yoke? Are the separate parts put together the chariot? Is it something other than its parts put together? Milinda cannot but say no to all these questions. Then replies Nagasena,

> Then for all my asking, Your Majesty, I can find no chariot. The chariot is a mere sound. What then is the chariot? Surely what Your Majesty has said is false! There is no chariot!

Milinda replies that just the parts put together is what is conventionally called the 'chariot' and that the word is merely a 'practical designation' to refer to these parts. To which Nagasena replies that just like the components of the chariot happened to be called 'chariot' due to convention, for practical purposes, so its aggregates together are called 'Nagasena'. So there's no such thing called the self, since not only is the self identical with any of the *khandas*, but there's nothing else apart from them. One's name is just a convention to designate a collection of parts, and yet, it's still a name for that very reason.

What makes this interesting is that the denial of the self's existence deals pretty well with multiple personality, split-brain cases and Teletransporter and fission cases. Parfit[xx] says that we don't have to think of many selves in split-brain cases because there are only mental states like the awareness of something without there being a self that is aware. Just like there can be a single state of awareness of many experiences, like hearing a bell ring and seeing a raven fly past a bell tower, in split-brain cases, there can be two states of awareness. That's it. There are just two states of awareness and no self, so these cases aren't really puzzling. We can extend that to multiple personality cases, too. Only awareness, no different selves in one body. There are just bundles of perceptions and feelings that exist in different streams of which we are aware.

In the Teletransporter case, the replica on Mars isn't me, and the one that remains on Earth isn't me either since there's no such thing as a self. I don't have to really fear if the original me is destroyed. In fission cases, there's no problem with transitivity since there's no self, so there's no x or y or z that can be identical with each other!

Not so quick perhaps. It was very strange that Milinda replied that the arrangement of parts isn't the chariot. It looks like it is the arrangement and the structure of the parts that make the chariot the chariot. But again, the arrangement cannot be the chariot since the parts can still change but the chariot remains. It looks like the chariot is what it is so long as it fulfils our purposes,[xxi] so indeed, the 'chariot' is just a practical designation based on our purposes.

But the disanalogy with the self perhaps lies here. Marya Schechtman says that the problem that plagued Parfit in trying to come up with a criterion for personal identity that isn't circular comes from thinking of the person as an object, like a tree or a human body. But the intuitions that we have regarding cases like fission and the Teletransporter come from us thinking of the person as a subject of experience. The reason he gets mistaken is because he tries to analyse personal identity in terms of something else, as if the self has detachable parts like an object. You can't give criteria that are used for objective objects in the world, which have detachable parts, like even the human body, for a subjective subject of experience.

If we look at the chariot again, we realize the problem. The chariot is an object with parts. Nagasena says that it doesn't exist and that the aggregate of parts is called a 'chariot' only relative to our purposes. If we think of the self as an object, of course, we will only find parts but no object called the self. This is what Hume seems to be looking for, too – some sort of object. But if the self isn't thought of as an object with parts but as the subject of experience, it exists. What is its nature and what enables it to persist?

The Soul Theory

Maybe this subject of experience is the soul, which is non-material and separate from the body. Not only does the soul not have parts, but it's also what is unchanging and bears all the changing properties like perceptions, sensations and feelings. The Soul Theory would say that:

x at time t_1 is the same as y at time t_2 if and only if x and y have the same soul.

This is a cool theory. The fission case would be dealt with because either the original soul gets annihilated or it goes to Lefty or Righty. We might not know to whom, but it's possible it's in one of them. Whoever has the same soul is identical with the original person. In the multiple personality case, one of them has the soul of the original Christine Beauchamp. Same with the Teletransporter. The soul either goes into the replica or doesn't, but we don't know. If it's there, then the replica is identical with the original. If Sita gets into an accident and gets total amnesia, it's Sita even though the memories get wiped out because the soul is the same.[xxii]

One major objection is this.[xxiii] The soul cannot be seen, tasted, felt or heard. Someone might judge that because a person has similarity of behaviour and character over time, or even the body, the soul is the same. But it's possible that since the soul can't be perceived, there's no reason why the soul doesn't change from moment to moment in a person. There might be different souls which are similar psychologically, and we have no way of knowing the difference. It doesn't follow that just because the behaviour and character or even mental states are similar, that the soul has to be the same. A river that is a particular river because it has murky water doesn't have to have the same water. Just as the water can be different and yet similar, the soul can be different at each time but the behaviour be similar. Even when it comes to my own soul, if it exists, I can have a soul in me for five years that's replaced after that, and I'll have no way of knowing it.

More importantly, souls seem to explain people's behaviour, thought, consciousness and emotions. However, if the brain explains all these, it's just unnecessary to invoke the soul to explain the same phenomena. well. There's a major problem with the existence of the soul, given what we have in modern science.

If the soul isn't the subject of experience, what is? It's time for you, the subject of experience, to start thinking at time t_1 and come up with an answer at time t_2!

WHAT IS ART?

In 1952, at the Maverick Concert Hall in New York, the pianist David Tudor started his stopwatch, sat down in front of the piano and shut its lid. Silence for thirty seconds, after which the stopwatch was reset, lid opened, closed again, then silence for another two minutes twenty-three seconds, lid opened, closed again, and then finally, silence for one minute and forty seconds. That was the controversial piece called '4'33"' by the composer John Cage. Yet there was music (supposedly) in the silence, the sound of rain on the rooftop, the breeze, people shifting and breathing. One point behind this was to get people to directly perceive the essence of life.

But is it art? In the twentieth century, a great many works were made to challenge traditional conceptions. Even in the twenty-first, you can see a banana taped to a wall with duct tape. Called *Comedian* and done by the artist Maurizio Cattelan, it was sold for 6.2 million dollars in an auction at Sotheby's to the crypto boss Justin Sun. Sun conveniently ate the banana at a press conference. Was it art? As a result of these types of challenges, the question of the definition of art became quite the challenge in the twentieth century.

An Ancient Look at Art

In Ancient Greece, Plato and Aristotle did not have our concept of art in the sense of the fine arts but looked at what we understand as the fine arts as crafts. Their word for it was *technê*, meaning 'skilful production', which also included weaving, woodwork and works created by craftsmen in general. And what we understand as the fine arts were imitative arts to them. Poetry (which included drama), music, painting and sculpture consisted of imitation. They didn't have a proper definition of art. But we can say that imitation had to be a necessary condition of art even though they didn't explicitly spell it out.

Plato, in his *Republic*, thought that art is imitation, which means that art simulates appearances. The world around us that we perceive with the senses is the world Plato thought to be the world of appearances. The real world, for Plato, is a world that is outside space and time, a permanent world containing Forms. Forms for Plato are the essence of each thing. For instance, what is common to all instances of beauty – that which makes beauty what it is – is its essence (we try to capture the essence of something by giving necessary and sufficient conditions, as you've already seen before). The essence of a triangle is that it is a closed plane figure with three straight sides. That's what makes a triangle a triangle. But these essences are not found in the world of appearances but in another world, which is the actual real world. These essences are called Forms.

One reason Plato believed this was that things around us aren't perfect. If you draw a triangle, the lines will never be perfectly straight (check that with a microscope!), and the line will not fit the definition of a line (it'll have some width, which a line isn't supposed to have since it is a series of points). So we never really perceive a perfect triangle. But we still perceive the imperfect figure that was intended to be a triangle, although it is an imperfect imitation of the perfect triangle. As a result, the reason we can still see the figure as an imperfect imitation of a triangle is because there exists a perfect triangle that we already had an idea of, which is something that cannot be perceived by the senses. That's why the essence of the triangle has to exist in a separate world outside the world that can be perceived by the senses.[i]

Plus, when we try to come up with definitions of *justice* and *beauty* and *virtue* or even a man, we only find that we can come up with particular instances of beautiful objects or just or virtuous actions. For example, when one asks what beauty is, one uses examples by pointing to beautiful objects and events like a sunset or a mountain. That still wouldn't explain what beauty is because the sunset and the mountain would have properties that would merely make each different from the other (for instance, the shape of the mountains versus the orange glow of the sun). So the properties of the sunset and the mountain are not what make them beautiful. The reason we experience the sunset as beautiful is because of the *Form of Beauty*, which lies in a different realm and that the sunset resembles the Form, which makes it beautiful.

For Plato, even beds and chairs and every object that we perceive has its essence in the realm of Forms: Bedness and Chairness. What is actually real is this realm of unchanging forms (beds will come and go, but the essence of a bed will be permanent and eternal). Knowledge involves a relation to an object, and knowledge is stable (since what we know will always be true). But if objects keep changing, by the time we come to know an object, it changes (even, for example, a molecule moves). If the object isn't stable, then knowledge of it won't be stable either. So, if knowledge isn't stable, then knowledge won't be possible. That's why, for Plato, there has to be perfect and permanent chairs and tables in an unchanging realm that we know, which explains why knowledge is stable.

Phew! Now what does this have to do with art? For Plato, the world of appearances is already away from reality. A painting, which is an image of something in the world of appearances, is twice removed from reality since it is the appearance of an appearance. Even music imitates, and what it imitates is the way people speak and speech patterns. That's why Plato didn't trust the dramatic poets and wanted to banish them from his ideal state – because appearances stirred up emotions, and this created unstable citizens.[ii]

Aristotle does believe that art imitates but in a different way. For Aristotle, the essences or Forms didn't exist in some separate realm but in things themselves. In his *Poetics,*[iii] imitation is not producing a likeness or copying reality but creating a semblance of reality produced by the imagination.[iv] The imitation is not of forms or everyday things but of how nature (human nature and non-human nature) works.

Imitation is an instinct in humans. Not only do we learn by imitation, but we also enjoy imitating things and learning through it. We might find something unpleasant when we see it directly, but we take pleasure when we see it in art. For instance, the sight of blood disgusts us. But when we see blood on Macbeth in Shakespeare's *Macbeth* after he has murdered Duncan, the king of Scotland, the blood gets transformed in our imagination. We understand its significance as a symbol of Macbeth's guilt and gain an insight into his feeling that his guilt cannot be wiped away at any cost.[v]

> 'What hands are here! Ha! they pluck out mine eyes.
>
> Will all great Neptune's ocean wash this blood
>
> Clean from my hand? No, this my hand will rather
>
> The multitudinous seas incarnadine,
>
> Making the green one red.'[vi]

In this way, we get to see the significance of things in art. For Aristotle, imitation in poetry (which includes drama) is not of things that have happened but of what can possibly happen. That is, events that are probable or that would happen inevitably. History deals with singular statements, that is, what a particular person with a particular name did. In doing so, it describes things as they have been. Poetry, on the other hand, deals in universal statements, describing what sort of thing something might be. So it looks at the sort of person. Because it shows us kinds of people, we get to learn about the nature of people. Tragedy then imitates noble actions and people, and comedy imitates the actions of the lowly and the ignoble. Plato and Aristotle are diametrically opposite in their view of art, even though they hold that imitation is key.

One major issue with the imitation view is that you can have architecture that is not an imitation or a representation of anything. A church building doesn't imitate or represent a house of God; it is a house of God. Another objection to this view is of things that have pure visual patterns and designs that don't represent anything. Also, Mark Rothko's paintings, some of which are just colours, don't imitate a colour; they are that colour or colours.

The Formalist View of Art

Due to the rise of movements in art in the last part of the nineteenth century, like Post-Impressionism, the focus moved away from representation to colour and the formal order of the painting. In light of this, paintings were not to be valued in terms of how well they represented things. The shift in focus was to the features of the painting itself.

Clive Bell, inspired by this movement, undertook to define art in his book titled simply *Art.*[vii] For Bell, even though different emotions arise as responses to different works of art, at bottom, they are of the same kind: aesthetic emotion. He looks at what is common to all works of art that leads to this aesthetic emotion, and this gives rise to his definition. His view, then, is that the quality that each work of art possesses is 'Significant Form', which is the way colours and lines are combined and related in art. We intellectually perceive how apt the form of a work of art is, how right and how necessary it is that the lines and colours should be arranged that way. It is because of this that we have aesthetic emotion. So X is a work of art if and only if it possesses significant form.

What art critics do is to help us observe the parts and the way they combine to give rise to significant form. For instance, a critic might point out the harmonious ways in which parts are combined in a painting. We might have missed out on such aspects, but we can now grasp the significant form and experience aesthetic emotion.

All this seems almost innocent at first glance. But aesthetic emotion is so specific to art that we don't feel it (or hardly ever feel it unless we project art into nature) when it comes to non-art, including even natural beauty. What we feel when we see a field of sunflowers is radically different in kind from the sort of emotion we experience when we see Van Gogh's painting of a field of sunflowers. In fact, for Bell, 'beauty' means 'desirable' to a man when he sees a beautiful woman and has more of a sexual connotation than an aesthetic one.

This might sound wild because you might say that, of course, there are beautiful pictures and paintings, poetry and music. But here, Bell makes a distinction between 'descriptive paintings' and works of art. Illustrations and portraits that might have psychological or historical valuc are descriptive paintings. We might be really interested in or even admire them, but they won't move us the way artworks do. What they do is 'suggest emotion' or convey information. What suggesting emotions means is that it is not that artworks are the objects of emotion, but they stir memories of emotions we have felt before. The suggested emotion is an everyday emotion, like the sadness we would feel at the death of a person. The object of an aesthetic emotion is an artwork, the object of a suggested emotion is the event depicted by a work of art.

Bell gives William Powell Frith's *Paddington Station* (1862) as an example of a descriptive painting. The painting, for Bell, is not a work of art because the lines and colours are arranged in a way that convey ideas and anecdotes and even suggest emotion but don't move us as a work of art. This doesn't have significant form.

So what about beautiful pictures, poetry and music? Bell says that we call the picture of a girl beautiful because it is the picture of a girl (so it's not that the picture is beautiful but the girl is, and it's conveying information about the girl). We call a piece of music beautiful, because, for instance, it stirs up emotions when we watch a musical farce with young ladies in it. And we call a poem beautiful because it reminds us of our feelings for some woman in our youth.

What all this implies is that representation in visual art, unlike what we saw in Plato and Aristotle, is irrelevant when it comes to its artistic merit. This doesn't mean representation doesn't have value. It does – but only in terms of form and not its content (that is, its subject matter). Bell does somewhat acknowledge the value of representation, and for him, significant form also includes space, which is representational, like in architecture, but it's not essential to art. The problem with representation is that if art is used merely to convey information and suggest emotion, then it cannot be distinguished from photographs and the cinematograph, which had emerged at the time Bell was writing. Their emergence had made the function of imitation in art obsolete and unnecessary. You can gain a lot more information through photos. And why bother with so much hard work to represent the world in a painting when it can be done automatically? In fact, Bell's whole argument is that the essence of visual art cannot be captured in terms of representation. Representation is not a sufficient condition for a work of art because, just because something represents, like a cartoon in the newspaper or a statue of Mickey Mouse in Disneyland, it isn't art. So representation is too broad a criterion because it'll count as art things that aren't. It's not a necessary condition either, since a lot of primitive art doesn't aim to imitate reality. You don't need an artwork to represent for it to be an artwork. Since representation (the content) fails as an essential quality of art, the argument goes, by elimination, form is.[viii]

How does an artwork have value in terms of the form? Bell says that for us to appreciate a work of art, we don't need to use our knowledge of life, its ideas and situations or even our familiarity with the emotions of life. Our experience of art is like the mathematician's, which is not a matter of representing the world but of sheer abstraction. He says:

> Art transports us from the world of man's activity to a world of aesthetic exaltation. For a moment we are shut off from human interests; our anticipations and memories are arrested; we are lifted above the stream of life.[ix]

It is this feature of art – that it possesses significant form and transcends the ideas that a particular age or culture brings to it – that makes it universal and permanently valuable. This is an advantage of Clive Bell's account of art, or so it seems.

One major objection to Bell's theory is that it is circular. The definition of significant form is the arrangement and combinations of lines, shapes and colours that give rise to an aesthetic emotion. And an aesthetic emotion is felt when significant form is perceived. Even if we talk about ecstacy or rapture in the presence of a painting, that cannot distinguish the aesthetic emotion from the ecstacy or rapture we would feel in non-aesthetic contexts. Bell has no option but to define aesthetic emotion in terms of significant form, which makes his definition circular. He has no independent criteria for defining either aesthetic emotion or significant form.

Another strong objection is that Bell's definition would exclude a great many significant works of art. You have lots of sculptures in Indian temples that are based on stories from the Indian epics. They, in fact, convey information. Their aesthetic value lies precisely in how well they depict these stories, and the form seems to be a tool to add to the effect of the stories and suggest the emotion associated with the stories.

Similarly, the Renaissance painting in the sixteenth century by Pieter Bruegel the Elder, *Landscape with the Fall of Icarus*, is based on a story from Greek mythology. The Athenian inventor and craftsman Daedalus and his son, Icarus, are imprisoned in a tower by King Minos of Crete. To escape, Daedalus makes himself and his son wings out of wax and warned him not to fly too close to the sun. But Icarus didn't heed this warning, and from overconfidence, flew too close to the sun. The wings melted, he fell into the sea and died. You can see a small part towards the front of the painting with Icarus' legs drowning near a ship, something which might escape notice. The painting conveys information that people are ignorant of other people's suffering even as they carry on with their lives. The value of the painting lies precisely in using the elements of it to convey this and suggest emotions associated with this. Bell's theory would exclude this painting!

Landscape with the Fall of Icarus -- After Pieter Brueghel the Elder, Public domain, via Wikimedia Commons

Art as Expression

Another attempt at defining art is: x is a work of art if and only if it is an imaginative expression of emotion. This theory is known as Expressionism. Thinkers like Leo Tolstoy, John Dewey and R.G. Collingwood held this view. Right now, we'll look at the British philosopher R.G. Collingwood's view, which he laid out in his book *Principles of Art* (1938).[x]

This feels like a view that people hold when they say that in making a work of art, you are expressing yourself, while some may say you are venting out your emotions. They might be onto something, but everyday uses, in Collingwood's view, can be somewhat confused.

Let's see what 'expressing an emotion' means for Collingwood. A person might have a vague feeling, but the person doesn't know exactly what it is. When this occurs, the person is in a 'helpless and oppressed condition'. The artist works out and explores this emotion through a self-reflective process and thus clarifies it. For instance, the poet does it through language, a painter through painting and a dancer through dance. In the process, the artist becomes conscious of the nature of the emotion and feels light and relieved as a result, escaping the oppressed condition. The relief is like when we express ourselves in angry words while being angry. The anger doesn't go away but persists, and yet, we are relieved since we are conscious of it. We were helpless when the anger was vague and unknown. But since it now sort of makes sense, we are relieved. The clarification and working out of this vague, undefined emotion is called 'expression' by Collingwood. From a very general awareness of a feeling like sadness, the artist comes to understand and express the unique sadness that is felt.

Not only does the creator become conscious of the emotion through expressing it, others, too, can become conscious of the emotion in the artist and in themselves. In fact, as a result of appreciating the artwork imaginatively, viewers recreate the artwork in their minds, expressing the emotion and becoming artists in the process. The reason art is valuable is because it enables both the creator and the viewer to clarify and understand their unique emotion.[xi] Collingwood says:

> This experience of the spectator's does not repeat the comparatively poor experience of a person who merely looks at the subject; it repeats the richer and more highly organised experience of a person who has not only looked at it but painted it as well.[xii]

Think of the swirling stars in Van Gogh's famous painting *Starry Night*. The viewer experiences the same organized and specific feeling that Van Gogh felt in creating it.

The Starry Night – By Vincent van Gogh - Google Arts & Culture - bgEuwDxel93-Pg, Public Domain, https://commons.wikimedia.org/w/index.php?curid=25498286

For Collingwood, there can be improper uses of the word 'expression'. First, expressing an emotion is not the same as describing it. Saying, 'I am angry' is describing my feelings of anger. On the other hand, expressing an emotion doesn't have to refer to the emotion. That's why the general advice while writing poetry is to avoid directly describing emotions (like using the word 'sad'). What describing does is to say that something is of a particular kind and classifies that thing – like classifying this emotion that I am feeling as anger. Expression brings out the particularity of the emotion itself, the specific anger I might feel at a certain time and towards a particular person and for a specific reason. Second, expressing an emotion is not the same as betraying an emotion. If I turn pale due to fear or shout and turn red due to anger, I am not expressing my emotion but betraying it. Unlike expression, I don't get clarity regarding the emotion when I am betraying it.

This understanding of expression, for Collingwood, brings him to the distinction between art and craft. An emotion is not expressed to arouse a feeling in others but to understand it. When I am expressing it, it is primarily addressed to me and only secondarily to the listener (or the viewer). This attitude is not like the attitude of someone who wants to arouse an emotion in another person. If one has the attitude of wanting to arouse an emotion in an audience, since they would know what is likely to arouse the emotion, they would use language and other means to do so in a specific way. But when it comes to expressing an emotion, the end (goal) isn't foreseen or pre-planned. The person is exploring an emotion he doesn't know and wouldn't know beforehand the right way to bring about the end, which is clarity of understanding.

So, there is a distinction between art and craft. Craft necessarily involves a means–end relation, as well as technique. The prevailing theory of art before Collingwood was the technical theory (*technê* in Greek is also skill, craft, expert knowledge), which involved Plato's and Aristotle's views, too. This view held that an artist is a skilled producer and the artwork is a means to produce certain emotions in an audience. This is what Collingwood goes against. He says that creating art doesn't have to have a clear means–end relationship or even technique. He's not saying that it doesn't involve technique at all. He's saying that the artist, a lot of times, just doesn't know what is going to be the end result beforehand, and the right means to bring that about isn't very clear either. The end result is not the arousal of emotion in the audience. It's just that the audience happens to overhear the artist who expresses emotion.

In Collingwood's view, amusement art, which is not art proper, involves the arousal of pleasure in the audience. Hitchcock movies would be considered by Collingwood as this sort of art, where Hitchcock consciously manipulated the camera, montage soundtrack and very specific techniques to generate emotions in his audience. This sort of entertainment is valuable for Collingwood, but it's not art proper.[xiii]

Another aspect of Collingwood's theory is that an artwork exists in the mind of the creator and the audience without having to exist in tangible form. For instance, the sounds or notes written on a piece of music on paper aren't the tune. The tune is in the creator's head, as well as in the audience's, and the soundwaves in the air or the notes are just a means of reconstructing the tune in the head. The medium – pain, clay or writing – is just a means for the audience to reconstruct an artwork, which can exist purely in their heads.

One criticism of Collingwood is that imaginative expression is not a sufficient condition for something to count as art. On his definition, the interaction between a psychotherapist and their client, which involves and leads to the clarification of an undefined emotion, would also be counted as art. Therefore, the theory would include too many things as art, which should not be so. It would also exclude many forms of art, including a great deal of religious art. A lot of religious art is created to arouse very specific religious feelings. But if we go by Collingwood's theory, they would be excluded as art. Art as expression is therefore not a necessary condition also because you can have religious art that is not an expression of emotion in Collingwood's sense.[xiv]

The Aesthetic Definition of Art

We saw that Clive Bell's formalist theory of art looked at features of artworks based on which he attempted to define art. Let's look at another theory that doesn't look at art in terms of features of the artwork but in terms of the experience it gives rise to.

When it comes to art, our experiences involve a contemplative state, which, as we saw Bell describing it, involves a freedom from concern with practical goals. The experience is thus different from the sort we have, for example, when we are filling an Excel sheet with data. In the presence of art, our perceptions, thoughts, beliefs, impulses, desires and feelings get elevated, which is tough to put into words, and the experience is an *aesthetic experience*. Having such an experience involves the 'exhilarating sense of exercising powers of discovery, integration of the self and its experiences'.[xv] When we visit museums to look at works of art, we tend to look at the works of art with the intention of having an aesthetic experience, and this is called an *aesthetic interest*. We have aesthetic interest because we consider the aesthetic experience to be valuable and rewarding. In light of this, Monroe Beardsley defines art as follows:

> x is a work of art if and only if (1) it is produced with the intention of making it possess a capacity in order to (2) satisfy the aesthetic interest (that is, fulfilling the intention of having the aesthetic experience).

The argument for the aesthetic definition of art is that since artists are interested in their works having audiences and that audiences take an interest in artworks to have these experiences, then the best explanation we have of this connection between artists and audiences is that the artists actually intend that the works have the capacity to satisfy aesthetic interest. See the analogy: People buy paint to paint their houses, and shops keep paint for people who have this goal so they can get what they are interested in. The best explanation for the nexus between paint manufacturers, shops and people is that paint makers intend by making paint to create the sort of thing that will fulfill the goals of people who need paint.[xvi]

How does this lead us to an insight into the nature of art? Given that there is such an intention from the artist and interest from the audiences, the nature of art is evident here – artworks must be the sort of thing produced with the intention of giving rise to aesthetic experiences.

The 'intention' in this instance is a mix of desire and belief: the desire to create a work to satisfy aesthetic interest and the belief on the part of the artist that the work that is being created or has been created is this sort of work. Also, there are degrees of satisfaction of the aesthetic involved, so the intention has to have the desired effect to some degree at least.

Beardsley's view has an added advantage over Expressionism since this intention doesn't have to be the only intention while producing an artwork; there might be a religious intention, too. So unlike Expressionism, you can create a work of art with the goal of invoking religious or political emotions.

An interesting feature of Beardsley's theory is that he says the impulse to produce an object in order to give rise to satisfying aesthetic interest is a primal impulse, even before traditions and institutions of art came up. That's why, the aesthetic theory includes children's poetry, artwork and music as art, something they create even before they get caught up in art institutions. In fact, psychologists have found this impulse in children to create pictures for aesthetic reasons.

One issue, on the face of it, with the theory is that if intentions are private, how does one classify something as a work of art, given that it'll be difficult to figure out the intention? One way to do this is through the evidence of the properties in the artwork. For instance, if there's a religious work to inspire devotion, we can look at the care with which the colour, the harmonies, variations in light, etc., have been composed.

One objection to the aesthetic definition of art is that suppose a toaster or a coffee cup has been produced with the intention of satisfying aesthetic interest. In this definition, the toaster and coffee cup will be works of art. This sounds a bit unpalatable, and the definition will be too broad and count too many things that aren't artworks as artworks. Thus, the definition doesn't provide a sufficient condition for what counts as art since just because something fits the definition, it won't be sufficient to count it as art.

Let's run through another objection that attempts to show that the definition doesn't give a necessary condition for something to be an artwork. In 1917, Marcel Duchamp gave in a urinal he bought from J.L. Mott Iron Works to an exhibition by the newly formed Society for Independent Artists (of which Duchamp himself was a founding member). He inverted the urinal and signed R. Mutt on it. The artwork is what we know as *Fountain*.

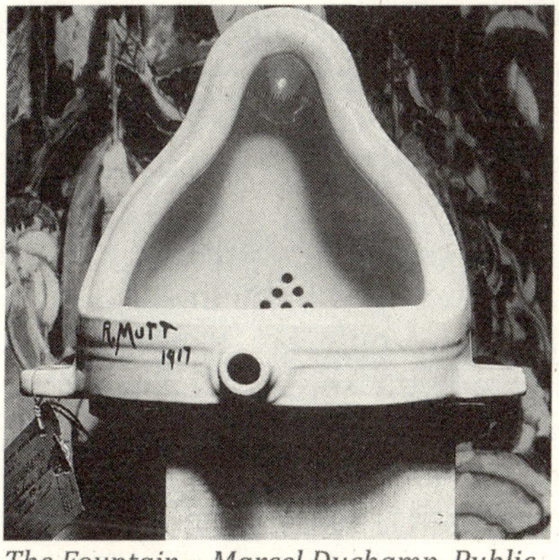

The Fountain – Marcel Duchamp, Public domain, via Wikimedia Commons

What was interesting is that the Society was an avant-garde group, questioning the existing ways in which artworks were selected. The Society held that they would never reject a work by any of its members. To test how well they would hold on to their principles and the extent of their tolerance, Duchamp submitted it. They rejected it, counting it as crude, and consequently, violated their own principles, and Duchamp resigned as a result.

Now Beardsley says that this was not really art since there was no intention to produce something with the capacity to provide the satisfaction of aesthetic interest. This was kidding art, merely called art but actually not so. Because otherwise, even ransom stamps and science exhibitions will have to be art. The problem that is typically seen with Bearsley's view is that, in fact, *Fountain* and other anti-aesthetic art ought to be counted as art. This is because, if we don't do so, then the definition doesn't actually take account of actual ways in which art has been classified, and artworks like this have been classified as art for eighty-five years by experts and informed viewers.[xvii] Thus, the aesthetic definition doesn't provide a necessary condition for what it is to be art since something can be a work of art without there being an intention to arouse aesthetic experience. You can think more about this case because it's one of those instances that provides a genuine puzzle as to what art is.

Can Art Have a Definition?

Maybe all this trouble regarding the definition of art is happening because art actually cannot be defined using necessary and sufficient conditions. People are logically confused because they don't understand the sort of concept art is. Morris Weitz in his 1956 paper 'The Role of Theory in Aesthetics' wrote that art is an 'open concept', that is, that the conditions under which the concept of art is applied can keep getting revised and corrected. For instance, we saw that *Fountain* challenged the very concept of art before it, because of which the concept of art expands to include further things. And given that the concept of art keeps expanding, it has to be open to the permanent possibility of change and of including novel items that might not be previously thought of as art. That's why, you can't define it, since if you did, it won't be expansive in the way it is, and that would limit creativity. This is in contrast to a concept that is closed, like that of a definition of a triangle, where one can give necessary and sufficient conditions for its application. And just like it is logically impossible to define bachelors as married adult males because of the very concept of bachelor, it is logically impossible to define art because of the nature of the concept of art.

One objection to this argument is that one can always say that the previous conceptions of art that new movements respond to are based on narrow definitions. It is still, in principle, possible to come up with a broad enough definition of art to include all movements and any new development. So Weitz's argument doesn't necessarily show that 'art' is an open concept even if limited conceptions of art keep changing. It can be a closed concept with a really broad definition.[xviii]

Another argument that Weitz gives for the impossibility of art having a definition is that when we come across a novel artwork, it is because of its resemblance to previous typical instances of artworks (paradigmatic works) rather than necessary and sufficient conditions. For Weitz, the concept of art is more like the concept of a 'game', which doesn't involve a definition. The famous philosopher Ludwig Wittgenstein looked at games and showed that you can't really come up with necessary and sufficient conditions for defining games.[xix] For instance, suppose you say that all games are amusing. Chess comes as a counterexample since it isn't. So being amusing isn't a necessary condition for being a game. Do they involve win and loss or competition for players? Solitaire is a card game that doesn't involve these. Or a child playing football with a wall. Suppose you try to define them in terms of skill. Well, ring-a-ring-a-roses doesn't involve it! Do games involve rules? One, that's not a sufficient condition, because just because there's a rule, it doesn't mean there's a game being played since lots of other activities in life involve rules.

As a result, the concept of 'game', for Wittgenstein, is a family resemblance term involving overlapping similarities but no common set of features that'll lead to necessary and sufficient conditions. Family resemblance is a metaphor based on how in a family, you don't need to have the same set of features for all members to be a part of the same family. One brother may share a similar nose with his father, the sister her eyebrows, and another brother may have his mother's eye colour but not the hair colour. In a family, there is an overlapping of features. That's the case with games, too.

Weitz argues that since 'art' is a family resemblance term, like 'game', it cannot have necessary and sufficient conditions. That's why art can't be defined.

The problem that plagues this argument is that everything can resemble everything in some respect. My table is a material object and so is the *Mona Lisa*. The Taj Mahal has a foundation but so does the building of my local grocer. Suppose we had to specify what a relevant resemblance is for a work to be counted as art, how do we emphasize the relevant resemblances and separate them from the differences between the new work of art and the paradigmatic work?[xx] And if we specify which similarities in which respect will make it count as a work of art, then we're coming up with necessary and sufficient conditions again[xxi] because those similarities will be those conditions!

The Institutional Theory of Art

When we look at actual family resemblances, the resemblances are based on features that are visible to people who see them. But there can also be properties that are not evident on the face of it, like genetic connections between the family, that explain the family resemblances. We'll look at the theory that tries to define art in terms of properties that are not manifest in the artworks themselves.

For George Dickie, one of the major proponents of the Institutional Theory of Art, the first attempt at defining art is (iff is just short for `if and only if'):

> X is a work of art in the classificatory sense iff (1) x is an artifact, and (2) 'a set of the aspects of which has had conferred upon it the status of candidate for appreciation by some person or persons acting on behalf of a social institution (the artworld)'.[xxii]

There's quite a bit to unpack here. Bell, Collingwood and Beardsley's definitions define art in an evaluative sense. That is, whether something is a work of art has to do with it having some value for us, whether it has some worth in commanding our attention. But Dickie looks at art in a classificatory sense. His definition isn't looking at whether or not artworks have value, and it's neutral in that respect. It's looking at how we actually describe something as art, like an anthropologist would, even if it is really bad art or completely worthless.

Next, let's look at what an artefact is. An artefact is an object made by a human, especially keeping in mind a subsequent use. A poem or a statue is an artefact and is different from an object found in nature.

The second part of the definition involves a particular status being conferred upon an artefact. Just in the way a couple gets the legal status of being married in a particular legal system when they're pronounced husband and wife by a relevant authority within the social institution, an artefact gains the status of being a candidate for appreciation by members of the cultural system of the artworld. That's how the status is conferred by the relevant authorities within institutions. And appreciation doesn't mean a unique sort of aesthetic appreciation or aesthetic perception. Dickie is sceptical of these. What he means by appreciation lies 'in experiencing the qualities of a thing one finds them worthy or valuable'.

Now, what is the artworld? The artworld is an 'established system' that consists of the people who think they're members of it, not just art auctioneers, critics, artists and dealers. An artefact becomes a work of art because it has been christened (or named, to put it simply) by a member of the artworld, which is usually the artist but can be any member or members. The artworld is significant because there are practices and conventions that give members the ability to confer status. There's a knowledge of the history of art, what sorts of things have been counted and not counted as art in history and a mutual understanding regarding art that allows them to understand what it means to treat an object as art. Just in the way a marriage gains the status of a marriage in the context of practices and the authority of some people to confer the status, an artefact becomes an artwork when a member of the artworld treats it as a candidate for appreciation. Conferral can happen, for instance, when a work is set out in a gallery or performed in an auditorium. And notice that being a candidate for appreciation doesn't mean that it will inevitably be appreciated. It's just a candidate and it might be trashed or never ever be appreciated. That's why Dickie is neutral as to its value as art.

Dickie's theory accounts for cases like *Fountain*, which is an artefact. It also allows for ever-evolving art and allows for an ever-expanding creativity of new ways of creating art since, as long as they fit the definition, they're art. But what if Duchamp had put out a naturally occurring piece of driftwood he had found on the beach in the gallery? Dickie's definition would allow that to be art since, for him, the status of an artefact can be conferred on a naturally occurring object even if it hasn't been modified or worked upon by a human. If an elephant painted something, it can be considered art not because the elephant has worked upon it (because it's not an agent and cannot create an artefact), but because a human in an institutional setting of art would confer upon it the status of an artefact.

This sort of conferral on a found object of the status of an artefact really sounds weird and mysterious. That's one reason why Dickie abandoned the first version of the Institutional Theory. It is one thing to hold that status conferred by an authority leads to a couple being married or becoming the prime minister. But it's really bizarre how a process like the previous one can confer the status of an artefact, that is, something made by someone.[xxiii]

In light of this inadequacy, Dickie revises his view and says that a piece of driftwood can actually become an artefact when it's used as a tool to dig or as a weapon. Earlier, we saw that an artefact is an object made by a human, especially keeping in mind a subsequent use. The optional part of the definition – 'especially keeping in mind a subsequent use' – doesn't apply when you just pick up a piece of driftwood and use it as a weapon, since it's being used right then (you can also see an unaltered stone found with human fossils as artefacts, since there is evidence of use). And unlike objects that are altered and produced as complex object as an artefact from more simple ones, there's no such thing done with the driftwood. Its artefactuality then consists in it being used in a particular way. The driftwood becomes an artefact when displayed in a gallery and becomes a new complex object – the-driftwood-used-as-an-artistic-medium. Even in the case of *Fountain*, a new object comes into being (it's not the same urinal) – the-urinal-used-as-an-artistic-medium. As a result, artifactuality isn't being conferred. An artefact is in fact created within the framework of the artworld.

The other objection Dickie takes seriously against his first definition is Beardsley's objection that we can think of people conferring status and acting on behalf of formal institutions like the institution of marriage, state or a university. But the institution of art is an informal one, which is an 'established practice', Beardsley's objection goes. It seems mysterious how practices can be the source of authority, unlike formal institutions.

As a result of the problems with his first definition, he abandons the bits about 'conferred upon' and 'acting on behalf of' in his second definition. Dickie revises the bit about status conferral to say that the status of an artwork is achieved due to the creation of an artefact, which, as we saw, had to have the artworld as the background for its creation. He also removes the part about the artefact being presented as a candidate for appreciation since such appreciation can also be of well-crafted functional objects (like a toaster) or a great advertisement.[xxiv] Me presenting an ad to a person from the artworld wouldn't necessarily make it art. So Dickie just has a work of art being something that is 'presented' to certain people. This, then, is his second definition:

x is a work of art if 'it is an artefact of a kind created to be presented to an artworld public.'

He then goes on to define each part of the definition as follows:

> An artist is a person who participates with understanding in the making of a work of art.
>
> A work of art is an artifact of a kind created to be presented to an artworld public.
>
> A public is a set of persons the members of which are prepared in some degree to understand an object which is presented to them.
>
> The artworld is the totality of all artworld systems.

> An artworld system is a framework for a presentation of a work of art by an artist to an artworld public.[xxv]

To clarify more bits, let's look at the second clause, that an artwork is 'an artifact of a kind created to be presented to an artworld public'. An artist might think that his work is good enough to be presented to the public or doesn't intend to present it. It might look as if Dickie is wrong in saying that it's created to be presented. But look at the precision. He says that it is the *kind* of work made to be presented. In fact, if wasn't the kind to be created to be presented, there would be no point in the artist deeming it worthless to be presented.

But there's still a problem with this. It is possible for artworks to be created outside the artworld. For instance, the psychiatrist Hanz Prinzhorn (1886 – 933) collected artwork by the mentally ill. The work was characterized by spontaneity and immense creativity and free from the clichés of the prevailing art of the day.[xxvi] The people who created them didn't think of themselves as members of the artworld. Their work was thought to be more in touch with the springs of artistic creativity than work done self-consciously by contemporaries. In Dickie's theory, such work wouldn't be counted as art no matter how beautiful or intriguing. Oddly, on his theory, it'll become art only if a member of the artworld goes ahead, obtains these and presents it to the artworld public. This seems wrong.[xxvii]

Along similar lines, this view also ends up with a chicken–egg problem. If there can't be art without an artworld, which came first – the art or the artworld? Did they come up together? That sounds strange. Surely the art would have come first for the artworld to have come into existence. In that case, there can be art without there being an artworld.

Another objection is that Dickie's definition is circular. A work of art is defined as an artefact of the kind to be presented to the artworld, and the artworld public is a group of people to whom the work of art is presented. As you can see, an artwork is defined in terms of the artworld public, and the artworld public is defined in terms of a work of art. Dickie says that this isn't an issue for his view since, even though the definition is circular, it's not viciously so. The notions in the definition, according to him, depend on each other. For instance, we can see that we learn about art sometimes by learning how to be an artist, which in turn is learning how to make paintings to be presented. And learning how to be a member of the artworld public is just to learn how to understand pictures made by artists. We learn about the practice of art only by being immersed in it, like learning the rules of chess. You can't define art independently of this practice. So maybe at least here, he has a point.

My favourite objection is the one given by Richard Wollheim. Either there are good reasons why members of the artworld would confer the status of art to an object or there are no good reasons, and it has been considered art at a whim or arbitrarily. Or if you want to think in terms of the second of Dickie's definitions – there must be a good reason to create an artefact within the background of the artworld or not. If there are reasons, like form or an innovation in form in the context of the history of art, beauty or themes in the artwork that we find worth contemplating, then we can actually have a theory of what art is, and that won't be the institutional theory. We can use such reasons as part of a theory of art. And if there are no such reasons, then the work of art has its status arbitrarily. Dickie's reply might be that the objection is smuggling in evaluative concepts while his task is to understand what classifies it. But since his theory doesn't explain why we value art, it still looks like we can't find reasons why something should be part of the institution, and in fact, we do deliberate on these matters seriously.

A Naturalist Definition of Art

The philosopher Denis Dutton considered the need for art to be an evolutionarily evolved instinct. But the reason he called his definition of art a naturalist one was not because of biology but because there was cross-cultural behaviour and discourse regarding the way art is made, experienced and assessed. Based on cross-culturally universal characteristics of typical art, he sets out what he calls recognition criteria for art. These aren't necessary and sufficient conditions, but we'll see how they form part of a definition.

Direct Pleasure

The artwork provides an aesthetic pleasure, that is, the story or the performance is valued because it provides immediate pleasure, and this experience is valuable for its own sake. The artwork is not valued for its utility, like we would value a knife for its utility in cutting something. Nor is it valued because it leads us to something else that is pleasurable. This pleasure can be gained from the way a tight plot falls into place (which is like the pleasure from a good chess problem) or the way a pattern of harmony and rhythm occurs in music or the composition of a painting. This is not a sufficient condition for art because you can even have this kind of pleasure when you play tennis or cricket. And it's not necessary either, since a work that doesn't give pleasure might still be art.

Emotional Saturation

Artworks are saturated with emotion in two senses. First, artworks themselves can have an emotional flavour: There's a certain emotional tone to a novel or a musical symphony. Second, there's also the emotion experienced by the audience because of the representational content: the sense of pathos in the tragic scene of a play, the emotion felt while watching a funny scene in a comedy or sadness while viewing a sad painting. This isn't necessary since there can be minimalist artwork that doesn't involve such emotion. It's not sufficient either since we can experience emotions when we fall in love, at the death of a loved one, at the birth of a child, etc.

An Indian View on Art

The Nāṭyaśāstra was an ancient Indian treatise on drama (which also includes music and dance), said to be authored by Bharata but written over three centuries from 200 to 500 CE. It says that the main goal of drama is to give rise to rasa (Sanskrit term meaning 'taste', 'juice', (flavour'). Rasa is the emotion an audience experiences by the performance.

This emotion is not merely an ordinary emotion or experience involving taste but is characterized by 'self-forgetfulness'. Abhinavagupta in his eleventh-century commentary says that the experience takes one away from a concern with one's own emotion and towards appreciating a universal type of emotion. Thus, rasa isn't valued for its utility. There is also another emotion, bhava, which is the emotional tone of the drama, the emotion represented by it. Stāyibhāva is a durable emotion and a core aspect of human experience, which is the emotion that dominates the emotional tone of a work. This tone can be a result of various emotions in the work itself. There are eight of these mentioned by the Nāṭyaśāstra: 'erotic love (rati), mirth (hāsya), sorrow (śoka), anger (krodha), energy (utsaha), fear (bhaya), disgust (jugupsa) and astonishment (vismaya)'.[xxviii]

The stāyibhāvas are produced by people, objects, plot, theme and circumstances and the like in a play (vibhāvas or determinants), expressions of feeling like gestures and behaviour (anubhāvas or consequents) and transient moods (vyabhichāribhāvas or complementary psychological states) that contribute to the experience of the stāyibhāvas. There are thirty-three of these moods,

> and some of these conditions are joy, agitation, impatience, stupor, weakness, discouragement, etc. If a transient mood becomes dominant, then there is no rasa. For instance, a sentimental or pretty artwork (found often in drawing rooms) will have a transient emotion that dominates. In this case, as David Hume (1777–1776) says, 'There is a species of beauty, which, as it is florid and superficial, pleases at first; but being found incompatible with a just expression either of reason or passion, soon palls upon the taste, and is then rejected with disdain, at least rated at a much lower value.'[xxix]
>
> There are eight rasas in the Nāṭyaśāstra:'[xxx]the erotic (śṛṅgāra), the comic (hāsya), the pathetic (sorrowful) (karuṇā), the furious (raudra), the heroic (vīra), the terrible (bhayānaka), the odious (bībhatsa) and the marvellous (adbhuta). Tranquillity or quiescence (śānta) was the ninth one added to the list by commentators.

Skill or Virtuosity

The artwork is a result of considerable skill. People specialize in this skill either because they have been apprenticed or because they had talent and learnt it along the way. It can be the skill of a writer, painter, sculptor, composer or any sort of artist and needn't be merely intellectual. It's the sort of skill that is admired and can even move people to tears or give them goosebumps. Again, this is not a sufficient condition since we might admire the skill of someone who breaks a record. It's not necessary either, since *Fountain* wasn't admired for this sort of technical skill.

Style

Performances, as well as art objects, have their own styles, that is, there are norms and rules of composition, form or expression that govern them. In the way that all our meaningful activity that goes beyond autonomic reflexes like gestures, the way we use language, manners, our bodily distance from people operate within a certain stylistic framework that contains norms, style gives a stable framework that allows for predictability. In this background, artists can either conform or break the rules to innovate and be liberated from it. Styles may come from the culture, a family or be invented by individuals. Again, not a sufficient condition because other activities involve style, too.

Novelty and Creativity

We value artworks because they can be original, novel and can surprise us. Dutton says that creativity includes the function art has to grab our attention and the artist's ability to delve into new ways a medium or a theme can be taken. Again, creativity can be seen in other areas like cooking or engineering, so this isn't a sufficient condition.

Criticism

With respect to artworks, there is a critical language that involves evaluation and appreciation of artworks. The language can be simple and less developed as in preliterate societies or as elaborate as the one in literature departments at universities in modern societies. Evaluation can be done by the people who create art, professional critics, as well as audiences. There is criticism typically involved in other fields like politics or religion, too, where the standards for what counts as success are complex and open-ended. Again, that's why this is not a sufficient condition.

Representation

People take pleasure in the way a painting, sculpture, novel or even music at times imitate actual and possible ways in which the world and humans are. There can be pleasure in the skill of the representation, for instance, the realistic way in which the folds have been made by Bernini in *The Ecstasy of Saint Teresa*. People also take pleasure in the excellent way the saint is represented, too. This sort of pleasure can be taken in other things that represent, like maps and illustrations in a newspaper.

Ecstasy of Sain Teresa – By Gian Lorenzo Bernini – Own work, CC BY-SA 4.0, https://commons.wikimedia.org/w/index.php?curid=43527951

Special Focus

Artworks across cultures are made the special focus of attention by them being set apart from the mundane course of events. This is called 'making special' by the evolutionary anthropologist Ellen Dissanayake. Works of art are foregrounded and brought into focus by a grand stage, high price for tickets, fancy book covers, plinths, the formal attire of the orchestra, a decorative frame and other such means. We can also find this special focus in religious rituals, presidential ceremonies and even sports like the opening ceremonies of the Olympics.

Expressive Individuality

Art expresses the individual personality of the artist. In activities where the outcome is well-defined, like accountancy, there's no scope for this sort of expression. Even in non-literate cultures where the works might not look so personalized or the work isn't signed, people know the individual artists and value their talent and expressive personality. Again, individual expressiveness is valued in cooking, advertising, teaching styles and other such areas, too.

Intellectual Challenge

Art challenges our perceptual and intellectual capacities and even stretches them beyond their limits. For instance, working out the complex themes and analysing characters in a complex novel, or trying to solve a complex murder mystery while the detective is trying to solve it too or teasing out the complex strands in a poem and figuring the significance of each line. Of course, again, you can find intellectual challenges in everyday life, like a crossword puzzle or a quiz.

Art Traditions and Institutions

As we saw in the Institutional Theory of Art, people understand what artworks mean in the context of the artworld. This is because there are traditions and institutions in small and large cultures in which works of art are understood and gain their significance. Almost all social activities like medicine, sports, education and warfare happen in the background of traditions and customs.

Imaginative Experience

This is considered by Dutton most likely to be the most important characteristic of artworks. Art involves an imaginative experience, which differentiates it from sports like football, which also involve skill, emotion, pleasure and special focus. When I look at a painting, there exist only blobs of paint on the surface, but I experience the image through imagination. Listening to a story is an imaginative experience and so is the experience of harmony in sound patterns. In fact, all art involves the imagination and is a necessary feature of art. Activities apart from art, like planning, forming a hypothesis and daydreaming also involve the imagination, so imaginative experience is not a sufficient condition for art.

Now the reason Dutton sees these criteria as a definition even though all may not be present when we encounter a work of art is because these are disjunctive criteria, that involve either x or y or z and so on between each item on the list. Some criteria are more important, like skill, virtuosity and imaginative experience, but criticism isn't that much when it comes to recognizing a work of art.

The most interesting thing about Dutton's approach is that he doesn't start out with hard cases like *Fountain* and then try to define art, unlike the Institutional Theory. He starts out with obvious and central cases. And his theory explains why borderline cases are hard precisely because it is so tough to fit them into the recognition criteria. For instance, even cooking can be a hard case because criteria like skill and producing pleasure might make us want to include it as art. But because cooking doesn't involve emotional saturation, intellectual challenge and representation, it might make us want to exclude it.

Now what might you think about *Comedian*, the one with the banana and the duct tape using these criteria? Is it art?

References

Getting Started

[i]Julian Baggini, *Making Sense: Philosophy Behind the Headlines* (New York: Oxford University Press, 2002).

[ii]Wilfrid Sellars, 'Philosophy and the Scientific Image Of Man', in *Science, Perception and Reality* (London: Routledge & Kegan Paul, 1963).

[iii]Arthur S. Eddington, *The Nature of the Physical World* (New York: Macmillan, 1928).

[iv]William L. Craig, *The Kalam Cosmological Argument* (London: Macmillan, 1979), 63

[v]Robert Kirk, *Relativism and Reality: A Contemporary Introduction* (1st ed.) (Routledge, 1999).

[vi]Justin P. McBrayer, 'Why Our Children Don't Think There Are Moral Facts' (2015). https://archive.nytimes.com/opinionator.blogs.nytimes.com/2015/03/02/why-our-children-dont-think-there-are-moral-facts/?mcubz=0

[vii]Michael Huemer, *Knowledge, Reality and Value* (2021)

The Meaning of Life

[i]A. Camus, *The Myth of Sisyphus* (Penguin UK, 2013).

[ii]Francis T. Palgrave, *Palgrave's The Golden Treasury* (Good Press, 1905/2022):301.

[iii]Richard Taylor, 'The Meaning of Human Existence', in *Introduction to Philosophy: Classical and Contemporary readings*, eds. Perry, John, Michael Bratman and John Martin Fischer (Oxford University Press, 1993).

[iv]William Shakespeare, *The New Clarendon Shakespeare: Macbeth* (Oxford University Press, 1939) :110.

[v]Thomas Nagel, 'The Absurd', *The Journal of Philosophy*, 68 (20) (1971): 716–727.

[vi]Susan Wolf, 'Life, Meaning Of', in *The Routledge Encyclopedia of Philosophy* (Taylor and Francis, 1998).

[vii]Epicurus, *Letter to Menoeceus*, trans. Robert Drew Hicks (2016).

[viii]Robert Nozick, *Examined Life: Philosophical Meditations* (Simon and Schuster, 1990).

[ix]Jean. P. Sartre, (2001). Existentialism. *From Existentialism and Human*

Emotions by Jean-Paul Sartre, translated by Bernard Frechtman, A Philosophical Library Book, Citadel Press. Reprinted in Cahn, Steven. M. (2018). *Exploring Philosophy: An Introductory Anthology.* Oxford University Press

[x]Stephen P. Stich, *Philosophy: Asking Questions—Seeking Answers,* ed. Tom Donaldson (New York: Oxford University Press, 2018).

[xi]Susan Wolf, 'Happiness and Meaning: Two Aspects of the Good Life', *Social Philosophy and Policy, 14* (1), (1997): 207–225.

[xii]*Ibid.,* 209.

[xiii]*Ibid.,* 212.

[xiv]Susan Wolf, *Meaning in Life and Why It Matters* (Princeton University Press, 2010).

[xv]*Ibid.*, p. 94 from Jeanne Nakamura and Mihaly Csikszentmihalyi (2003) The Construction of Meaning through Vital Engagement. In *Flourishing: Positive Psychology and the Life Well-Lived,* eds. C.L.M. Keyes and J. Haidt (Washington D.C.: American Psychological Association: 83–104; p. 87.

[xvi]Jay Garfield, *The Meaning of Life: Perspectives from the World's Great Intellectual Traditions. Lectures from The Great Courses* (2013).

[xvii]*The Bhagavad Gita,* trans. Eknath Easwaran (New Delhi: Nilgiri Press, 2007):23.

[xviii]Stephen Phillips, *Yoga, Karma, and Rebirth: A Brief History and Philosophy* (2009).

[xix]*Ibid.*

[xx]Keya Maitra, *Philosophy of the Bhagavad Gita: A Contemporary Introduction* (New York: Bloomsbury Academic, 2018).

[xxi]Tuvia Gelblum, 'On "the meaning of life" and the Bhagavad Gita', *Asian Philosophy* 2 (2) (1992): 121–130.

[xxii]A. Kumar and S. Kumar, '*Karma* Yoga: A Path Towards Work in Positive Psychology', *Indian J Psychiatry* 55 (Suppl 2) (2013): S150–2.

[xxiii]*The Nicomachean Ethics,* ed. Leslie Brown (USA, 2009).

[xxiv]Susan Wolf, *Meaning in Life and Why It Matters* (2010), 97–98.

[xxv]Jonathan Haidt, *The Righteous Mind: Why Good People Are Divided by Politics and Religion* (2012).

[xxvi]Jonathan Haidt, *Religion, Evolution, and the Ecstasy of Self-Transcendence* ((2012), YouTube. Available at: https://www.youtube.com/watch?v=2MYsx6WArKY&t=923s (Accessed: 09 February 2024).

[xxvii]Jonathan Haidt, *The Righteous Mind: Why Good People Are Divided by*

Politics and Religion

[xxviii]*King James Bible* (1769/2008).

Morality

[i]Ruth Benedict, 'Anthropology and the Abnormal' *Journal of General Psychology* 10 (2) (1934): 59–82.

[ii]*Ibid,* 71.

[iii]Harry J. Gensler, *Ethics: A Contemporary Introduction* (New York: Routledge, 1998).

[iv]Bernard Williams, *Morality: An Introduction to Ethics* (New York: Harper & Row, 1972).

[v]Mary Midgley, 'Trying Out One's New Sword' in *Heart and Mind: The Varieties of Moral Experience* (London: Routledge, 1981).

[vi]Harry J. Gensler, *Ethics: A Contemporary Introduction.*

[vii]Joel Feinberg, 'Psychological Egoism' in *Reason and Responsibility* (Encino, Calif.: Dickenson Pub. Co, 1971).

[viii]John Stuart Mill, *Utilitarianism,* ed. Geraint Williams (Cleveland: Cambridge University Press, 1863).

[ix]Michael Bruce and Steven Barbone, (eds.) 'Mill's Proof of Utilitarianism' in *Just the Arguments* Fyfe, A.T. (Wiley-Blackwell, 2011).

[x]Judith Jarvis Thomson, 'The Trolley Problem', *Yale LJ*, 94, (1984): 1395.

[xi]Peter Singer, 'Famine, Affluence, and Morality', *Philosophy and Public Affairs* 1 (3) (1972): 229–243.

[xii]This Malthusian stuff on population reduction leading to famine reduction is pretty wrong. In fact, despite there being an increase in population from one billion in 1800 to seven billion plus today, people dying today in famines has reduced to a fraction. https://ourworldindata.org/famines?s=09

[xiii]Onora O'Neill, 'The moral perplexities of famine relief', in *Matters of Life and Death*, eds. Tom L. Beauchamp and Tom Regan (Philadelphia: Temple University Press, 1980).

[xiv]Julia Annas, 'Virtue Ethics', in *The Oxford handbook of ethical theory,* ed. David Copp (New York: Oxford University Press, 2006): 515–536.

[xv]James Rachels and Stuart Rachels, *The Elements of Moral Philosophy,* 9th edition (New York: McGraw-Hill, 2019).

[xvi]Rosalind Hursthouse, 'Virtue Theory and Abortion', *Philosophy and Public Affairs* 20 (3) (1991): 223–246.

[xvii]*Ibid*, 235.

[xviii]Christopher Gowans, *Philosophy of the Buddha: An Introduction* (Routledge, 2003).

[xix]Padmasiri De Silva, (2017) 'Buddhist Ethical Theory' in *Indian Ethics: Classical Traditions and Contemporary Challenges: Volume I,* eds. Purushottama Bilimoria and Joseph Prabhu (Routledge, 2007).

[xx]Fiery Cushman and Liane Young, 'The Psychology of Dilemmas and the Philosophy of Morality', *Ethical Theory and Moral Practice* 12 (1) (2009): 9–24.

[xxi]Joshua Greene, 'The Secret Joke of Kant's Soul', in *Moral Psychology*, ed. W. Sinnott-Armstrong, Vol. 3. (Boston: MIT Press, 2007).

[xxii]Michael Huemer, *Knowledge, Reality, and Value: A Mostly Common Sense Guide to Philosophy* (Kindle Edition, 2021).

[xxiii]Michael Koenigs, Liane Young, Ralph Adolphs, Daniel Tranel, Fiery Cushman, Marc Hauser and Antonio Damasio, 'Damage to the prefrontal cortex increases utilitarian moral judgements', *Nature* 446 (7138) (2007): 908–911.

Free Will

[i]Harry G. Frankfurt, 'Freedom of the Will and the Concept of a Person', *Journal of Philosophy* 68 (1) (1971): 5–20.

[ii]Susan Wolf, (1987). 'Sanity and the Metaphysics of Responsibility' in *Responsibility, Character, and the Emotions: New Essays in Moral Psychology*, ed. Ferdinand David Schoeman (1987): 46–62.

[iii]David Widerker, 'Libertarianism and Frankfurt's Attack on the Principle of Alternative Possibilities, *Philosophical Review* 104 (2) (1995): 247–61.

[iv]Peter Van Inwagen, 'The Incompatibility of Free Will and Determinism', *Philosophical Studies*, 27 (3) (1975): 185–199.

[v]Robert Kane, *A Contemporary Introduction to Free Will* (New York: Oxford University Press, 2005). (I owe a lot to this book for this chapter.)

[vi]Michael McKenna, 'Compatibilism', in The Stanford Encyclopedia of Philosophy, online edition, ed. Edward N. Zalta: http://plato.Stanford.edu/archives/sum2004/entries/compatibilism/. As cited by Robert Kane, *A Contemporary Introduction to Free Will* (New York: Oxford University Press, 2005).

[vii]Bahar Gholipour, 'A famous argument against free will has been debunked', *The Atlantic*, 10 (2019).

[viii]Robert Kane, 'Responsibility, Luck, and Chance', *Journal of Philosophy,* 96

(5) (1999): 217–240.

[ix]Harry. D Potter and Kevin J. Mitchell, 'Naturalising Agent Causation', *Entropy,* 24(4) (2022): 472.

What is Knowledge?

[i]Edmund L. Gettier, 'Is Justified True Belief Knowledge?' *Analysis* 23 (6) (1963): 121–123.

[ii]George B.J. Dreyfus, *Recognizing Reality: Dharmakirti's Philosophy and its Tibetan Interpretations* (Albany, NY: SUNY Press, 1997). As quoted in Jonathan Ichikawa and Matthias Steup, 'The Analysis of Knowledge', *Stanford Encylopedia of Philosophy* (2017).

[iii]M. Clark, 'Knowledge and Grounds: A Comment on Mr. Gettier's Paper', *Analysis* 24 (2) (1963): 46–48.

[iv]R.G. Meyers and K. Stern, 'Knowledge Without Paradox', *The Journal of Philosophy 70* (6) (1973): 147–160. As quoted by Richard Feldman, 'An Alleged Defect in Gettier Counter-Examples', *Knowledge: Readings in Contemporary Epistemology,* eds. Sven Bernecker and Fred I. Dretske (2000).

[v]Richard Feldman, An alleged defect in Gettier counter-examples, *Australasian Journal of Philosophy* 52 (1) (1974): 68–69.

[vi]Alvin I. Goldman, A Causal Theory of Knowing, *Journal of Philosophy* 64 (12) (1967): 357–372.

[vii]Goldman's example is from Carl Ginet.

[viii]Robert Nozick, 'Knowledge', *Philosophical Explanations* (Cambridge: Cambridge)

[ix]Robert Audi, 'Introduction: A Narrative Survey of Classical and Contemporary Positions in Epistemology', *Epistemology: Contemporary Readings*, ed. Michael Huemer (2002).

[x]Saul A. Kripke, 'Nozick on Knowledge', in *Philosophical Troubles. Collected Papers Vol I.* (New York: Oxford University Press, 2011).

[xi]Keith Lehrer and Thomas Paxson, 'Knowledge: Undefeated Justified True Belief', *Journal of Philosophy* 66 (8) (1969): 225–237.

[xii]The details of their account are more complicated but this sort of summarizes it.

[xiii]As pointed out by Thomas Grundmann, 'Defeasibility Theory' in *The Routledge Companion to Epistemology,* eds. Sven Bernecker and Duncan Pritchard (2011): 156–166.

[xiv]Alvin I. Goldman, 'What is Justified Belief?' in *Justification and Knowledge: New Studies in Epistemology,* ed. George Pappas (Boston: D. Reidel 1979): 1–25.

[xv]Rodrigo Borges, 'Gettier and Externalism', in *The Gettier Problem,* ed. Stephen Cade Hetherington (New York: Cambridge University Press, 2018).

[xvi]Laurence Bonjour, 'Externalist Theories of Empirical Knowledge', *Midwest Studies in Philosophy* 5 (1) (1980): 53–73.

[xvii]Laurence Bonjour, 'Internalism and Externalism', in *The Oxford Handbook of Epistemology,* ed. Paul K. Moser (New York: Oxford University Press, 2002): 234–264.

[xviii]Linda Zagzebski, 'The Inescapability of Gettier Problems', *Philosophical Quarterly* 44 (174) (1994): 65–73.

[xix]C. Starmans and O. Friedman, 'Expert or Esoteric? Philosophers Attribute Knowledge Differently Than All Other Academics', *Cognitive Science* 44 (2020): e12850.

[xx]*Ibid*, 14.

[xxi]*Ibid*, 14.

[xxii]*Ibid*, 14.

[xxiii]This is George Pappas and Marshall Swain's definition quoted by Zagzebski.

[xxiv]Jaysankar Lal Shaw, (2015). 'The Relevance of Indian Epistemology to Contemporary Western Philosophy', in *Comparative Philosophy and J.L. Shaw,* eds. P. Bilimoria and M. Hemmingsen. Dordrecht: Sophia Studies in Cross-Cultural Philosophy of Traditions and Cultures 13: 83–101.

Skepticism

[i]John Cottingham, ed., *Descartes: Meditations on First Philosophy: With Selections From the Objections and Replies* (New York: Cambridge University Press, 1996).

[ii]Hilary Putnam, *Reason, Truth and History* (New York: Cambridge University Press, 1981).

[iii]These examples are from Jonathan Vogel, 'Skepticism and Inference to the Best Explanation', *The Norton introduction to philosophy,* eds. Gideon Rosen, Alex Byrne, Joshua Cohen and Seanna Valentine Shiffrin (New York: WW Norton & Company, 2015).

[iv]I'm modifying it slightly so it seems like a direct response to Vogel.

[v]G.E. Moore, 'Proof of an External World', *G.E. Moore: Selected Writings* (New York: Routledge, 1993), 147–170.

[vi]Nigel Warburton, *Thinking from A to Z* (London: Routledge 2013).

[vii]Example adapted from John Turri, *Epistemology: A Guide* (Hoboken: Wiley-Blackwell, 2013).

[viii]Crispin Wright, '(Anti-)Sceptics Simple and Subtle: Moore and McDowell', *Philosophy and Phenomenological Research,* 65 (2002): 330–48.

[ix]Hilary Putnam, *Reason, Truth and History.*

[x]Crispin Wright, 'On Putnam's Proof That We Are not Brains-in-a-Vat', *Reading Putnam,* eds. P. Clark and B. Hale (Oxford: Blackwell, 1994).

[xi]Keith DeRose, 'Contextualism and Knowledge Attributions', *Philosophy and Phenomenological Research*, 52 (4) (1992): 913–929.

[xii]Richard Feldman, 'Contextualism', *Blackwell Companion to Epistemology,* eds. Matthias Steup, Jonathan Dancy, and Ernest Sosa, (West Sussex, UK: Blackwell, 2010).

[xiii]Alvin I. Goldman and Matthew McGrath, *Epistemology: A Contemporary Introduction,* ed. Matthew McGrath (New York: Oxford University Press, 2014).

[xiv]Earl Conee, 'Contextualism Contested', *Contemporary Debates in Epistemology*, eds. in Matthias Steup John Turri (Chichester, West Sussex, UK: Blackwell. 2013), 47–56.

[xv]Fred I. Dretske, 'Epistemic Operators', *Journal of Philosophy*, 67 (24) (1970): 1007–1023.

[xvi]Krzysztof Sękowski, Adrian Ziółkowski and Maciej Tarnowski, 'Western Skeptic vs Indian Realist. Cross-Cultural Differences in Zebra Case Intuitions', *Review of Philosophy and Psychology* 14 (2) (2021): 715-716.

[xvii]Rene Descartes. (1853). The Meditations, and Selections from the Principles of Philosophy, of Descartes. Translated from the Latin, and Collated with the French; with Preface, Appendix, and Notes [John Veitch, Trans.]. Sutherland & Knox: 19.

[xviii]The discussion on this issue is entirely from Kisor Kumar Chakrabarti, 'Nyāya's Response to Skepticism', *International Journal for the Study of Skepticism* 12 (1) (2021): 72–89.

[xix]Vātsyāyana, *Nyāyabhāṣya,* 74

[xx]*Ibid,* 74.

[xxi]*Ibid,* 74.

Personal Identity

[i]Paul Broks, *Into the Silent Land: Travels in Neuropsychology* (London: Atlantic Books, 2003).

[ii]John Locke, 'Of Identity and Diversity', in *An Essay Concerning Human Understanding*, section II.27, ed. Peter H. Nidditch (Oxford: Clarendon Press 1689).

[iii]Thomas Reid, 'Memory' (Essay 3), in *Essays on the Intellectual Powers of Man.*

[iv]Sydney Showmaker, 'Personal Identity: A Materialist's Account' in *Shoemaker*, Sydney and Swinburne, Richard. *Personal Identity* (Oxford: Blackwell, 1984).

[v]Derek Parfit, 'Personal Identity', *Philosophical Review*, 80 (1971): 3–27.

[vi]Joseph Butler, 'Appendix I', in *The Analogy of Religion* (1736).

[vii]Helen Beebee and Julian Dodd, eds., *Reading Metaphysics: Selected Texts with Interactive Commentary* (2007).

[viii]Marya Schechtman, 'Personhood and Personal Identity', *Journal of Philosophy* 87 (2): (1990) 71–92.

[ix]Bernard Williams, 'The Self and the Future', *Philosophical Review* 79 (2) (1970): 161–180

[x]John Perry, 'Williams on the Self and the Future', in *Identity, Personal Identity, and the Self.* (2002),103–118.

[xi]Brian Garrett, 'Personal Identity', in *The Routledge Encyclopedia of Philosophy*. (1998).

[xii]Eric T. Olson, 'Personal Identity' in *Blackwell Guide to Philosophy of Mind,* eds. Stephen P. Stich and Ted A. Warfield (2002).

[xiii]Eric .T. Olson *'An Argument for Animalism',* in *Personal Identity: Blackwell Readings in Philosophy, eds.* Raymond Martin and John Barresi (2003).

[xiv]Stephan Blatti, 'Animalism'. *The Stanford Encyclopedia of Philosophy* (Fall 2020 Edition), ed. Edward N. Zalta, (2020). <https://plato.stanford.edu/archives/fall2020/entries/animalism/>.

[xv]Kathleen V. Wilkes, 'Multiple Personality and Personal Identity'. *British Journal for the Philosophy of Science*, 32 (4) (1981): 331–48.

[xvi]Susan Blackmore, *Consciousness: A Very Short Introduction* (2005).

[xvii]David Fate Norton & Mary J. Norton. (eds.) (2007). David Hume: A Treatise of Human Nature: Volume 1: Texts. Clarendon Press: 165.

[xviii]Ainslie. T. Embree, *Sources of Indian Tradition: From the Beginning to 1800* (1988):106.

[xix]Edward Craig, *Philosophy: A Very Short Introduction* (2020).

[xx]Derek Parfit, (2009) 'Divided Minds and the Nature of Persons', in *Science Fiction and Philosophy: From Time Travel to Superintelligence*, ed. Susan Schneider (2009), 91–98.

[xxi]Edward Craig, *Philosophy: A Very Short Introduction*.

[xxii]Michael Huemer, *Knowledge, Reality and Value* (2021).

[xxiii]John Perry, *A Dialogue on Personal Identity and Immortality* (1977).

What is Art?

[i]Plato applies this to 'Equality' rather than a triangle in his dialogue *Phaedo*. Plato, *The Last Days of Socrates: Euthyphro, Apology, Crito, Phaedo*, trans. H. Tredennick, H. Tarrant (Harmondsworth: Penguin, 1954, 1993).

[ii]Plato, *The Republic*, trans. C.D.C. Reeve (Indianapolis: Hackett, 2004).

[iii]Malcolm Heath, (trans.) *Aristotle: Poetics* (Harmondsworth: Penguin, 1996).

[iv]Schaper Eva, *Prelude to Aesthetics* (London: Routledge, 1968).

[v]C. Brooks, *Understanding Poetry* (Rinehart and Winston).

[vi]William Shakespeare. The New Clarendon Shakespeare: Macbeth (Oxford University Press, 2016): 50.

[vii]Clive Bell, Art, (London: Chatto & Windus, 1914).

[viii]Noel Carroll, 'Clive Bell's Aesthetic Hypothesis', in *Aesthetics: A Critical Anthology*, eds. Dickie George, Richard Sclafani and Roblin, Ronald (St. Martin's, 1989).

[ix]*Ibid*, 80.

[x]R. G. Collingwood, *The Principles of Art* (New York: Oxford University Press, 1938).

[xi]Nigel Warburton, *The Art Question* (New York: Routledge, 2003).

[xii]Collingwood, *The Principles of Art*, 308.

[xiii]Warburton, *The Art Question*.

[xiv]Warburton, *The Art Question*.

[xv]Monroe Beardsley, 'An Aesthetic Definition of Art' in Peter Lamarque, *Aesthetics and the Philosophy of Art: The Analytic Tradition: An Anthology*, eds. Olsen and Stein Haugom (Hoboken, NJ: Wiley-Blackwell, 2019), 25

[xvi]Noël Carroll, *Philosophy of Art: A Contemporary Introduction* (New York:

Routledge, 1999).

[xvii]*Ibid.* 1999

[xviii]Warburton, *The Art Question.*

[xix]Ludwig Wittgenstein, *Philosophical Investigations,* ed. Tim Page (New York, NY, USA: Wiley-Blackwell, 1953). Edited by G. E. M. Anscombe.

[xx]Warburton, *The Art Question.*

[xxi]Thomas Adajian, 'The Definition of Art', in *Stanford Encyclopedia of Philosophy* (2018).

[xxii]George Dickie, *Art and the Aesthetic: An Institutional Analysis* (Ithaca, N.Y.: Cornell University Press, 1974), 34.

[xxiii]Christopher Janaway, ed. *Reading Aesthetics and Philosophy of Art: Selected Texts with Interactive Commentary* (Oxford: Wiley-Blackwell, 2005).

[xxiv]Janaway (2005)

[xxv]George Dickie (1984/97). The Art Circle: A Theory of Art. (Evanston, IL: Chicago Spectrum Press): 80-82.

[xxvi]Warburton, *The Art Question.*

[xxvii]Janaway, *Reading Aesthetics and Philosophy of Art: Selected Texts with Interactive Commentary.*

[xxviii]Kathleen Mary Higgins, 'Rasa', in *A Companion to Aesthetics,* 2nd edition, ed. S. Davis et al. (Oxford: Blackwell, 2007), 492.

[xxix]David Hume, 'Of the Standard of Taste', in *Essays, Moral, Political, and Literary* (Indianapolis: Liberty Press, 1857), 226–249.

[xxx]Higgins, 'Rasa', 493.

Index

This is an accessible and wide-ranging introduction to the main areas of philosophy. Throughout, Chakravarty uses engaging examples and thought experiments to bring ideas alive for the reader. The book is also noteworthy for its integration of Indian philosophy – ranging from the Bhagavad Gita to the Nyāya school – with the Western canon. Students and lay readers alike will find much to engage with in this little volume.

– Hrishikesh Joshi, University of Arizona, USA, and author of *Why It's OK to Speak Your Mind*.